Battlefields of Texas

Bill Groneman

Maps and Graphics by Rod Timanus

Republic of Texas Press

Library of Congress Cataloging-in-Publication Data

Groneman, Bill.
    Battlefields of Texas / Bill Groneman : maps and graphics by Rod Timanus.
      p.   cm.
    Includes bibliographical references and index.
    ISBN 1-55622-571-7
    1. Texas--History, Military.   2. Battlefields--Texas.   3. Battles--Texas--History.
  I. Title.
    F386.G74   1998
    355' .009764--dc21   97-43654
                                                CIP

Republic of Texas Press is an imprint of Wordware Publishing, Inc.
No part of this book may be reproduced in any form or by
any means without permission in writing from
Wordware Publishing, Inc.

Printed in the United States of America

ISBN1-55622-571-7
10 9 8 7 6 5 4 3 2 1
97-12

All inquiries for volume purchases of this book should be addressed to:
Wordware Publishing, Inc.
2320 Los Rios Boulevard, #200
Plano, Texas 75074
Telephone inquiries may be made by calling: (972) 423-0090
http://www.wordware.com

Contents

iv

To Ma and Mikey Novak

God and Texas
Victory or Death

—**William Barret Travis**

Acknowledgments

I would like to thank and acknowledge all of the following: My wife Kelly, son Billy, daughter Katie, Ma and Mikey Novak, and the Dalmatians Glennis and Dotty. My friend and editor from Republic of Texas Press, Mary Goldman, not only for her encouragement but also for her hospitality along with that of her husband Mel and son Brian. Russell and Dianne Stultz of Wordware Publishing and the rest of the staff. The staff of the Daughters of the Republic Library at the Alamo: Director Cathy Herpich, Martha Utterback. Jeannette Phinney, Warren Stricker, Elaine B. Davis, Linda Edwards, Charles R. (Rusty) Gamez, and Sally Koch, not only for their help but for always making it feel like "Old Home Week" whenever I invade their domain. From the Alamo, Alamo Historian and Curator Dr. Richard B. Winders, Dorothy Black, and Gus Martinez. Friends from the Western Writers of America: Jane Eppinga, Preston Lewis, and Byron Price. The Lockhart County Chamber of Commerce; San Augustine Chamber of Commerce; Nacogdoches Convention and Visitors Bureau; Brownsville Chamber of Commerce; Charles V. Humphreys of the Brady / McCulloch County Chamber of Commerce; José Tweedy of the Tom Green County Historical Commission; Cesa Espinosa of the Panhandle-Plains Historical Museum; Crystal Balcazar of the Van Horn Convention & Visitors Bureau; Mary L. Irving of the Railroad and Pioneer Museum; Shänta Kuhl of the Taylor Chamber of Commerce; Jody Morrison of the National Park Service's Denver Service Center; Jody Wright-Gidley, Curator of the Bell County Museum; Shelly Henly Kelly of the Rosenberg Library; Kinney County Chamber of Commerce; Doris Gatton of the Brazoria County Historical Museum; Walter E. Plitt III, Chairman of the Palo Alto National Committee; Joel Honeycutt, Blanco County Historian; John Anderson of the Texas State Archives; Alan Morris, Supervisory Park Ranger at Fort Davis National Historic Site; Egina Reyes of the Texas State Historical Commission; Doug Murphy, Palo Alto Battlefield National Historic Site; Maxine H. Reilly, Director of the Refugio History Museum; Virginia Shahan of Alamo Village; Bob Carrier of the San Antonio Living History Association. The staff of the Malverne Public Library for once again helping me set the record for the most books on inter-library loan. My friends Tom Lindley of Austin for sharing his expertise on the Battle of the Alamo and the Texas Revolution, Bob Strong of San Antonio for keeping me current on the latest information, and Lieutenant Bob Sarno of the New York City Fire Department for his Civil War knowledge. A special thanks to friends Rod Timanus for his artwork and encouragement and to his daughter Rebecca for sharing her father for a while. Also a special thanks to friends Dave Bowser and Lupe Ramos of San Antonio for Dave's encyclopedic knowledge of many Texas battles, especially those in and around Bexar, and for Lupe's patience in accompanying Dave, Tom Lindley, and me to the many battle sites in San Antonio.

Introduction

Texas is a land of dramatic history, proud traditions, and many symbols which represent that history and those traditions. One of the most prominent of these symbols is the display of the "Six Flags Over Texas." These are or were the banners of six nations which at one time laid claim to Texas. They include the flags of Spain, France, Mexico, the Republic of Texas, the Confederate States of America, and the United States of America. Absent from this collection are symbols of any of the Native American tribes which for a time roamed freely over the length and breadth of Texas. Native American tribes were not really ones for national symbols. To tribes such as the Comanche it mattered little whose flag flew over the land they traveled. For most of their history they were clearly in charge wherever they roamed. Their "flags" and those of many other Native American Peoples have symbolically flown over Texas.

In short, the Texas of today is a product of many cultures and national identities. Such a blend does not come easily, however. When a land as great and rich as Texas changes hands so many times, it does not do so peacefully.

Most people outside of the Lone Star State remember the Alamo, but that is about as far as their association of battles to Texas goes. Actually, nineteenth-century Texas was the theater of several wars and the scene of a number of pitched battles. Most of these conflicts were small by comparison to those which raged across the rest of the world during the 1800s. Yet despite their limited size some of these battles were especially significant. For instance, the Battle of San Jacinto in 1836 involved less than three thousand participants, yet it became the fulcrum point upon which a vast area of North America turned.

What follows are brief descriptions of some of the more important battles and battlefields of Texas. Also mentioned are some of the lesser battles and their locations. It is not intended as a comprehensive study of any of the battles or sites included nor is it an all-inclusive list. There have been many more battles and fights on Texas soil. Each deserve and many have already been the subject of book-sized studies. My intention is to bring together for the first time some of the battles which have shaped Texas history. Perhaps it will renew an interest in some of the less-remembered conflicts in Texas's past. It may also generate some interest in documenting and preserving the exact location of these battlefields. Primarily it is a guide for casual visitors or travelers across Texas who may enjoy stopping along the road somewhere to see where history (in these cases violent history) happened.

The locations of some of the battlefields of Texas are known. A few are marked by historical sites of varying degrees of quality. Other sites have been lost to urban growth or are inaccessible on privately owned land. Others have been lost to time and their exact locations only guessed at. Many sites are identified by Texas historical markers.

On a recent trip through central and east Texas I visited the few battlefields which do have some kind of historical sites. I also took the time to stop and read a number of historical markers. This can be a pleasant experience when traveling across Texas if you are in no particular hurry. It can also become a somewhat addictive and time-consuming pastime. Texas encompasses some 262,840 square miles, divided into 254 counties. Spread throughout these counties are over 11,000 historical markers (not counting memorial, plaques, statues, etc.). It can also be somewhat hazardous. The more obsessive travelers may find themselves zipping across two-lane highways in the face of oncoming traffic so as not to miss a marker on the other side. A word of caution is advised. Still, I recommend to native Texans as well as visitors to the Lone Star State to take the time and check out some of the markers. You may be surprised to see what dramatic events have taken place right where you are standing. Many of the markers identify a battle site or describe a certain battle. Some of them describe a battle or have information related to a battle but are located miles from that battle site. Some markers are in places other than where they are supposed to be located. Some have been relocated off private land to more accessible locations. Others are relocated by vandals or pranksters from time to time.

In describing the battles, I have avoided presenting them as stories of Texans defending their homeland against its enemies, since that is not always the case. The United States fought Mexico on Texas soil in 1846. Thirty years earlier Mexicans, Anglo-Americans, and Native Americans fought Spain. The United States Army fought a number of engagements against the Comanche and other tribes. The United States fought the Confederacy on Texas land. Texan revolutionaries, mostly from the United States, fought Mexico on Texas soil while Texas was still part of Mexico.

It is difficult to think of another state within the United States which has been fought over so jealously as Texas. Many of our states have been the scene of battles throughout our history. The locations of most of these battles are almost incidental to the larger struggle for the survival of the U.S. or for the control of a large portion of North American real estate. In the case of Texas, however, the possession or control of the state or territory or country itself is more often than not the prize.

In making a compilation such as this is, decisions had to be made as to what constitutes a battle and which events should be included or excluded. Along with its proud history, Texas also possesses an extensive record of violent confrontations. The line that separates these confrontations from actual battles is not always well defined. I have tried to include descriptions of battle or fights in which two organized forces (whether professional military entities or not) with some specific strategic objectives in mind faced off against one another. I have excluded feuds, riots, spontaneous eruptions of violence, raids, many small-scale skirmishes between settlers and Native Americans, and large-scale law enforcement operations. However, there are no hard and fast rules. Some confrontations that may not be battles in the strictest sense of the word may still find their way in. I have tried to include battles and fights that have sites that can be visited or at least identified. Some smaller confrontations are included since there are historical markers to identify the location.

Some of the battles are clearly part of a specific war such as the Civil War, the Mexican War, or the Texas Revolution. Others occurred during the time spans of certain wars but were not actually part of that war. For instance, the first Battle of Adobe Walls occurred in 1864 while the Civil War was in progress, but the battle had little to do with the War Between the States. Some of these battles produced tangible results, others did not. Some can be considered glorious, some heroic, some senseless, and others tragic. The history of Texas through the nineteenth century is part of the larger story of the expansion of the United States across the North American Continent. This expansion, whether it is called "Manifest Destiny" or "the winning of the West" or "the greatest land grab in history," relied a great deal on firearms. In keeping with the American frontier tradition of achieving ends through a proficiency in the use of guns, many of the battles of Texas are known for a "famous shot" or in some cases an "infamous shot." These are instances in which a single shot, whether by rifle, pistol, cannon, or in some cases bow and arrow, initiated a battle, changed the course of a battle, robbed one side of a valuable leader, or are noteworthy simply due to a fantastic act of marksmanship. Some of these will be described when they occur in any particular battle.

The battles are listed in chronological order, with the side that took the offensive or initiated the battle listed first. At the beginning of each entry, the opposing forces, their leaders, and the approximate size of their forces are given when known, in the following manner:

Opponents:

The force (or army, or units)

The leader(s)

The number of personnel involved

In almost all cases, numbers concerning the size of forces, casualties, survivors, etc. are approximate. Conflicting sources, lack of accurate documentation, and exaggeration with the passage of time give these figures a wide range. This is especially true with some of the more legendary battles.

In some cases I have listed sites, museums, libraries, or theaters which pertain to certain battles. I have tried to include the most recent hours of operation and admission prices for these locations. Since prices and hours of operation may change at any time, it is advisable to check with the specific site first.

Chapter One
Spanish/Mexican Texas

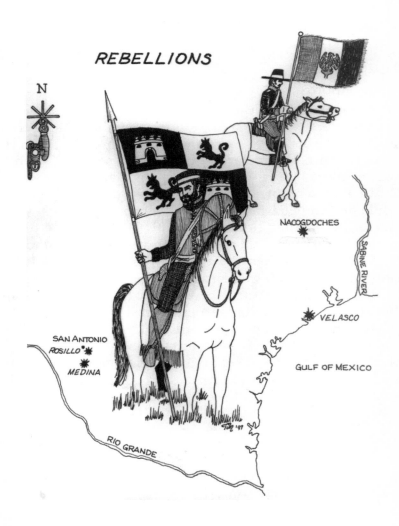

REBELLIONS

N

NACOGDOCHES

SABINE RIVER

VELASCO

SAN ANTONIO
ROSILLO
MEDINA

GULF OF MEXICO

RIO GRANDE

Cañon de Ugalde
9 January 1790

Opponents:

Spanish Royalist army; (Comanche warriors; Spanish civilians)

    Colonel Juan de Ugalde

       35 men

Lipan Apaches

    Approximately 300 men

Colonel Juan de Ugalde was one of Spain's fiercest Indian fighters, and his special target was the Apache tribe. In December of 1789 Ugalde was exploring the Texas Hill Country with a small group of Spanish soldiers when he discovered a large fortified village of Lipan Apaches.

Ugalde sent back to San Antonio de Bexar for help while he camped with Comanche allies. Over the next few weeks he accumulated a force of 44 soldiers, 140 Comanche warriors, and 51 Spanish civilians. On January 9, 1790, he attacked the village which was defended by approximately 300 warriors and 10 chiefs.

Ugalde's force routed the warriors from the village and burned it. The Apaches retreated north towards another village and joined up with a smaller group of their tribesmen. They continued their retreat along the west side of the Sabinal River and set an ambush on a bluff above the river. Ugalde's scouts located the trap and the Spanish were able to defeat and scatter the Apache warriors.

Casualties:

The Apaches lost two chiefs, twenty-eight warriors, twenty-eight women, and one child killed. Thirty women and children were captured. Ugalde's force lost three killed and four were wounded.

Outcome:

This battle dealt a serious blow to the power of the Lipan Apaches in central Texas and strengthened the position of the Comanches. It also impressed a number of Comanche chiefs who sought peace with the Spanish. Ugalde rescued fifteen Spanish captives as a result of this battle and seized almost eight hundred horses.

Location:

There is some debate over the location of this battle. It is believed to have taken place in an area which was known as "Arroyo de Soledad" in either the Sabinal Canyon, four miles south of Utopia, or in Dry Frio Canyon north of Uvalde. The area is in present-day Uvalde County about fifty miles west of San Antonio.

Markers:

There is a Texas historical marker commemorating "Uvalde County" on U.S. 90, 3.9 miles east of the town of Uvalde. It explains how the county's name evolved from that of the canyon named after Juan de Ugalde.

Rosillo
29 March 1813

Opponents:

Spanish Royalist Army

    Manuel Maria de Salcedo, governor of Texas

    Simón de Herrera, governor of Nuevo León

        950-1500 men

The Republican Army of the North

    José Bernardo Gutiérrez de Lara

    Samuel Kemper

        600-900 men

The Battle of Rosillo was one of the actions of the Gutiérrez-Magee Expedition, a filibustering expedition in which a coalition of Mexican citizens, Anglo-American adventurers and Native Americans sought to wrest Texas from Spain. This expedition is sometimes referred to as the "First Texas Revolution."

Spanish Royalist forces under Governors Salcedo and Herrera had besieged Republican forces under Augustus W. Magee in the Presidio La Bahia from early November 1812 to mid-February 1813. Salcedo finally ended the siege since he was unable to break the Republicans, and also due to losses and discontent among his own men. He returned to his base of operations in San Antonio de Bexar.

Magee died of fever during the siege, but by mid-March the expedition's new leaders, José Bernardo Gutiérrez de Lara and Samuel Kemper, reorganized the force and it set out for San Antonio. The force was a mixed bag of Mexicans, Americans, Couslatta, Lipan, and Tonkawa Indians, and even a few deserters from the Spanish force.

On the morning of March 29, they approached San Antonio from the south along the Mission Road. Their immediate goal was to reach the Mission San Francisco de la Espada and camp for the night. The Royalist force with

950-1,500 men and six brass cannon waited for the Republican force just above the fork of the lower (Mission) road and the upper road.

The ambush was revealed when a Royalist cannon fired on the right wing of the Republican force. The Republicans quickly deployed in a line parallel with the Spanish force approximately 500 yards away. The Americans of the force made up the middle of the line with the Native Americans on the right and the Mexicans on the left. The Spanish advanced slowly, firing cannon balls at the Republicans with little effect. The Republican force lay flat on the ground and waited for the attack signal which was to be one tap of a drum. The Spanish closed to within 100 yards when the signal was given. The Mexicans on the left and Native Americans on the right charged on horseback. The Americans struck the center of the Spanish line with one group specifically assigned to seize the cannon. The mounted troops on either wing caused the ends of the Spanish line to collapse on itself. With the Americans attacking them from the front and the mounted troops hitting them from either side, the Spanish force became unable to fight and incapable of flight. Spanish officers suffered many casualties trying to rally their demoralized troops. Many of the Spanish surrendered to the Americans and passed through their lines. Once behind them and with no one to guard them many of the Spanish soldiers took the opportunity to flee.

The battle ended in less than an hour with the Spanish force completely routed. The Republican force camped at the Mission Espada that night. On April 1 their force lined up in battle formation outside of San Antonio de Bexar. Salcedo, Herrera, and twelve other officers promptly surrendered rather than subject the town to a hopeless battle. Two days later these men were marched from Bexar by Antonio Delgado of the Republican force to a spot near where the battle took place and were brutally tortured and then beheaded. When news of this reached Bexar, Americans in the Republican force were horrified, and some rushed to the site to bury the dead. Afterwards many of the American troops "took furloughs" and returned to the U.S.

Casualties:

The Republican casualties at Rosillo were minimal, probably only five or six dead and wounded. The Royalist casualties are estimated at anywhere from one hundred to three hundred thirty with many taken prisoner.

Outcome:

Rosillo was a decisive victory for the revolutionary Republican Army of the North. It routed the Spanish force and captured a valuable store of arms and ammunition as well as over 1,500 horses and mules. As a result the first short-lived Republic of Texas was established. Unfortunately, the brutality after this battle set a precedent for many Texas battles to come.

Location:

The battle took place some miles south of San Antonio de Bexar in what is now Bexar County. The exact sites of the battle and the executions have never been confirmed.

Markers:

A somewhat damaged Texas historical marker stands on a remote intersection of W.W. White Road, Hildebrand and Cacias Streets just on the southeast city line of modern San Antonio.

Royalist officers executed after the battle of Rosillo:

Spanish

Governor Manuel Maria de Salcedo	
Governor of Nuevo Leon	Simón de Herrera
Lieutenant Colonel	Geronimo Herrera
Captains	Juan de Echeverria
	José Groscochia
	Francisco Peiera
	José Mateos
	Juan Ignatio Arambido
Lieutenant	Gregorio Amado

Citizen	Antonio Lopez

Mexican

Captain	Miguel de Areos
Lieutenant	Louis de Areos
Ensign	Francisco de Areos
Lieutenant	Juan Caso

Alazán
20 June 1813

Opponents:

The Republican Army of the North

　Major Henry Perry

　Approximately 650-900 men

Spanish Royalist Army

　Lieutenant Colonel Ygnacio Elizando

　　Approximately 3,000 men

On June 18, 1813, Lieutenant Colonel Ygnacio Elizando and his force of Spanish Royalists made their camp on the Alazán Creek about one-and-one-half miles northwest of San Antonio de Bexar. He had already exceeded his orders from General José Joaquín de Arredondo to wait for Arredondo and his force somewhere between the Frio and Medina Rivers. They were then to join forces and defeat the Republican Army of the North, which was still savoring its victory at Rosillo, in the comfort of Bexar.

Instead, Elizando proceeded to Bexar and sent three American prisoners into town with an offer for the Americans among the Republican force. The offer called for them to give up the Gutiérrez-Magee expedition and hand over certain Mexican rebels to the Spanish. In return the Americans would be guaranteed the pay due them for their service with Gutiérrez and they would be free to return to the U.S.

Lieutenant Colonel Reuben Ross, who had distinguished himself in the Rosillo battle, urged retreat with the assumption that Elizando would not pursue them. In lieu of that option he advocated taking cover in the old Alamo mission on the east side of the San Antonio River. His men adamantly refused to abandon the town, so Ross slipped away on his own in the middle of the night. He was replaced by Major Henry Perry, a relative of Commodore *Oliver H. Perry.

Major Perry called for an assembly of his troops on the morning of June 19, but not one of the Mexican troops of the Republican army joined the Americans. This seemed to confirm a rumor that the Mexican troops were considering selling out the Americans to the Royalists. The problem was resolved when Perry informed Miguél Menchaca, the commander of the Mexican and Tejano cavalry, that the Americans would hand over to Elizando the rebels he had requested, including Menchaca.

During that day the Republican force readied itself for action. It moved out sometime that night and by just before dawn it was poised and ready at Elizando's camp. The Royalists had set up camp on the rear of a deep ravine near a pool of water. They had constructed two bastions 400 yards apart and connected with a curtain wall. Two cannon were mounted on the left to protect the entrance of the ravine.

The Royalists were at morning prayers when the Republicans opened fire with their cannon. Elizando quickly positioned his infantry in the ravine and his few cavalry behind the cannon. The Republican artillery concentrated on the Royalist artillery and cavalry, dismounting one of their enemies' pieces and pushing the mounted troops back. The Royalists attempted to flank the Republican line on the left but were driven back. Finally, the Republicans left their cannon and charged the ravine, driving the defenders before them. A Royalist labor force armed only with short swords fought back with a barrage of stones they had piled up on the bank of the ravine. The Royalists moved back toward their bastions where they attempted to make a final stand. The Republicans moved forward, firing on them until they finally called for quarter. Elizando escaped with a portion of his force to the Presidio del Rio Grande. The battle lasted about four hours.

Casualties:

There are a variety of descriptions of casualties for this battle. Probably the best estimate lists the Republicans as losing four killed and twenty wounded, possibly five of whom died later. The Royalists are estimated to have lost 350 killed, and 130 taken prisoner, 52 of whom were wounded.

Outcome:

Alazán was another victory for the Republican Army of the North. The most significant result of the battle was that the Republicans re-equiped their whole force with the windfall booty they seized. This included 5,000 pounds of gunpowder; 350 stands of arms; 1,000 horses and mules with saddles; plus food, clothing, money, tents, baggage, and the two cannon.

Location:

This battle took place on the Alazán Hill, a long sloping ridge between the Alazán and Apache Creeks to the northwest of San Antonio de Bexar. This location is now within the city of San Antonio in Bexar County.

Medina
August 1813

Opponents:

Spanish Royalist Army

   General José Joaquín Arredondo

      1,830 men (635 infantry and 1,195 cavalry)

The Republican Army of the North

   General José Alvarez de Toledo y Dubios

      A variety of accounts differ, generally from 1,000 to 1,400 men

Following their defeats at Rosillo and Alazán, the Spanish Royalists sent a substantial force under General Arredondo against the Republican forces at San Antonio de Bexar. Gutiérrez had been court-martialed and relieved of command for his involvement in the executions after Rosillo. General José Alvarez de Toledo y Dubios, with U.S. backing, had been elected to lead the Republicans.

The Republican force became aware of Arredondo's force when the Royalists were about fifty miles south of Bexar. The Americans among the Republicans wanted to wait in town for the enemy. The Mexicans and Tejanos favored going out to meet them, thus sparing the town. Toledo decided to meet Arredondo south of Bexar.

On August 18, 1813, Toledo and his men were camped about six miles from the Royalists. He planned to ambush them along the Laredo Road. His troops were formed up at 8:00 A.M. in single file with Mexican and American companies alternated in the line, supported by six small cannon.

Arredondo sent Lieutenant Colonel Elizando from his camp at 5:00 A.M. with 180 cavalrymen to reconnoiter the Republicans. The "famous shot" of the battle of the Medina occurred when Alferés don Francisco Lopez drifted ahead of Elizando's force and was fired upon by the Republicans, thus revealing Toledo's ambush. The Republican force advanced on Elizando's men, who fought but gave ground before them. Arredondo ordered another 150 cavalrymen with two one-and-a-half-pound cannon forward to support Elizando. The Republicans mistakenly thought this was Arredondo's main force. They were further encouraged when the Royalists continued to retreat before them, even abandoning their cannon. Despite Toledo's efforts to restrain his men, the Republicans pressed their attack, exhausting themselves by dragging their cannon through the heat and sandy terrain without water. The mounted Royalists outdistanced their pursuers and led them directly into Arredondo's main force.

The Royalists opened up with their fourteen remaining pieces of artillery scattering the Republican force. The battle raged back and forth for about four hours. At one point a handful of Americans managed to silence all of the Royalists' cannon and force their line to give way. The Royalists drove back the Americans when it was observed how few in number they were. Finally, the Republicans broke and were completely routed. The Royalists pursued and slaughtered most of the Republicans who were wounded, had surrendered, or were too weak to flee. Toledo was one of the less than one hundred Republicans who managed to escape.

Casualties:

The Spanish Royalists lost 55 killed, 178 wounded, and 2 missing. The Republican force was wiped out with the exception of the less than a hundred who escaped and a handful who were taken prisoner and later escaped. More than one hundred prisoners who were not slaughtered on the field were later executed.

Outcome:

The Spanish Royalists won a bloody victory and avenged their losses at Rosillo and Alazán. More importantly they crushed the Gutiérrez-Magee expedition and ended the attempt to free Mexico and Texas from Spain. The battle also taught a young Royalist officer named

11

Antonio Lopez de Santa Anna the arts of war he would employ twenty-three years later.

The Probable Battlefield of the Medina in Atascosa County
(Photo by Dave Bowser)

Location:

The location of the Battle of the Medina has not been confirmed archaeologically. Bexar County claims the location. It is said to have taken place on the Medina River, several miles south of the present-day San Antonio city line. The book *Forgotten Battlefield of the First Texas Revolution* by Ted Schwarz and edited by Robert H. Thornhoff disputes this claim and makes a strong case for the battle to have been fought about ten miles further south, in Atascosa County on the Galvan Creek, rather than the Medina River.

Markers:

A badly vandalized Texas historical marker commemorating the Battle of the Medina stands at the intersection of U.S. 281 and FM 2537 in Bexar County.

Some of the Republican army's known survivors from the Battle of the Medina:

José Alvarez de
    Toledo y Dubios
Peter Boone
Aylette C. Buckner
Henry Adams
    Bullard
Goodwin B. Cotton
Gormley
Samuel Kemper
William McLane
George Orr
Henry Perry
Juan Mariano Picornel
José Francisco Ruiz
John Villars

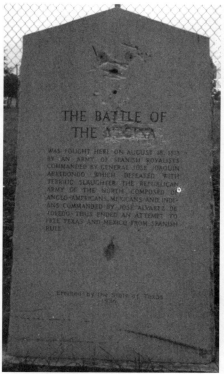

THE BATTLE OF
THE MEDINA

WAS FOUGHT HERE ON AUGUST 18, 1813
BY AN ARMY OF SPANISH ROYALISTS
COMMANDED BY GENERAL JOSÉ JOAQUIN
ARREDONDO WHICH DEFEATED WITH
TERRIFIC SLAUGHTER THE REPUBLICAN
ARMY OF THE NORTH COMPOSED OF
ANGLO-AMERICANS, MEXICANS AND INDI-
ANS COMMANDED BY JOSÉ ALVAREZ DE
TOLEDO. THUS ENDED AN ATTEMPT TO
FREE TEXAS AND MEXICO FROM SPANISH
RULE

Erected by the State of Texas
1936

El Perdido
19 June 1817

Opponents:

Filibustering expedition

    Colonel Henry Perry

        43 men

Spanish Royalist Army

    Lieutenant Colonel Juan Ignacio Pérez

Henry Perry led forces of the Gutiérrez-Magee expedition to victory at the Battle of Alazán but then suffered defeat with them at the Battle of the Medina in 1813. He fled to the U.S. and joined (or rejoined) the U.S. Army, possibly taking part in the Battle of New Orleans. He returned to Texas in 1816 with approximately two hundred and fifty men on another filibustering expedition, camping on what is now Bolivar Point. He left for Tamaulipas with an expedition under Francisco Xavier Mina in 1817 but became disenchanted with its possibilities of success. He broke off from the expedition with forty-three men with the goal of seizing La Bahia (Goliad). He arrived there on June 18 and demanded the surrender of the post. Lieutenant Colonel Juan Ignacio Pérez, the commander at La Bahia, had other plans.

As soon as Pérez and his men prepared for battle rather than surrender, Perry and his men lost heart and fled to the northeast. The Royalists caught up with Perry and surrounded his force the following day. Perry's small force was quickly defeated, and he committed suicide rather than fall into the hands of the Royalists.

Casualties:

Perry's expedition lost twenty-six men killed, including Perry himself.

Outcome:

El Perdido was a victory for the Spanish Royalist forces and a waste of life for another foolhardy filibustering expedition.

Location:

The Battle of El Perdido is believed to have been fought in a wooded area about one mile north of the present-day town of Fannin in Goliad County.

Markers:

A Texas historical marker indicating the "Site of Battle of El Perdido" is located on FM 2987, one mile north of Fannin in Goliad County.

Jones Creek
September 1824

Opponents:

Settlers from the Lower Brazos River

    Randal Jones

        23 men

Karankawa tribe

    Approximately 30 men

Raids against settlers by the Karankawa tribe prompted Stephen F. Austin to authorize a retaliatory raid led by Randal Jones. In September of 1824, Jones led twenty-three men down the Brazos River by water. At the mouth of the river they learned from a group of Karankawas that there was an encampment of their tribesmen about seven miles upriver. They also learned that ten to twelve Karankawas had gone to Bailey's store at Bailey's Prairie to obtain supplies and ammunition.

Jones sent two men to Bailey's to recruit some reinforcements and took the rest of his men back upriver to the Indian camp. The men who were sent to Bailey's found a group of settlers closely watching the Indians. The settlers convinced themselves that the Karankawas wanted the ammunition to use against them. The settlers opened fire on the Indians the next morning, driving them back to their camp.

Meanwhile, Jones had camped on the side of a creek, which would later be named after him, opposite that of the Karankawas. However, he could not determine the exact location of the Indians' camp. At sunset he was finally alerted to the location by the uproar when the Karankawas returned from Bailey's with their dead and wounded.

Jones and his men crossed from the east to the west side of the creek about a half mile above the camp. They attacked at daybreak, driving the Karankawas into the cover of the long grass surrounding their camp. The warriors quickly mobilized and soon had Jones and his men on the run back up the river, finally forcing them back to the east side. The "famous shot" of Jones Creek came when Jones turned to see an Indian preparing to shoot an arrow at him. Jones fired first and killed the warrior.

Casualties:

The Karankawas are believed to have lost fifteen men. The settlers are said to have suffered three killed and many wounded.

Outcome:

The Karankawas were driven across the San Bernard River, but hostilities still continued between the tribe and white settlers.

Location:

This fight took place on the banks of Jones Creek in southern Brazoria County, about half a mile from the present town of Jones Creek. The Karankawas camp was described as being on the west side of the creek where it widened into a lake before emptying into the San Bernard River. The site is on private land. The Brazoria County

Historical Museum and Research Center and the Brazoria County Library can provide information on this battle.

Brazoria County Historical Museum
   100 E. Cedar
   Angleton, TX 77515
   409-849-5711 ext. 1208
   Tuesday-Saturday 11 A.M.-5 P.M.
   Closed major holidays
   Admission: donations accepted.

Brazoria County Library
   412 N. Front
   Angleton, TX 77515
   409-849-5711 ext. 1505
   409-849-5711 FAX

Markers:

A Texas historical marker designates the site of the "Battle of Jones Creek." It stands on SH 36, nine miles west of the town of Freeport in Brazoria County. There is another historical marker in Corpus Christi at the intersection of Ocean Drive and South Alameda which gives a brief history of the "Karankawa Indians."

Chapter One

Calf Creek
21 November 1831

Opponents:

Tahuacano, Waco, and Caddo warriors
     Approximately 164 men
Civilians
    Rezin P. Bowie
       11 men

The Calf Creek Indian fight came about as a result of Rezin and James Bowie's search for the Los Almagres Silver Mines. These legendary mines were thought to be in the vicinity of the Santa Cruz de San Saba mission to the northwest of San Antonio de Bexar. The brothers and a party of nine others left Bexar on November 2, 1831. On November 19 the party was several miles north of the Llano River when they met two Comanches and a Mexican captive of theirs. They spoke for a while, and

James Bowie
From a protrait by George P.A. Healy. ca. 1831-34. (Courtesy of the Texas State Library and Archives Commission)

the companies parted and proceeded on their ways. On the following morning the Mexican captive returned to the Bowie party and warned them they were being followed by a large party of Tahuacano, Waco, and Caddo Indians. The Comanche chief sent word that he had unsuccessfully tried to dissuade these warriors from attacking the

18

Bowies. He also offered to try to protect the Bowie party with his eighteen men if they would return.

The Bowies declined the offer and proceeded on until they found a defensible campsite of thirty to forty thick oak trees, about forty yards from a stream. At 8:00 A.M. on November 21 the war party appeared. Rezin Bowie and David Buchanan went out to speak with them. When the two were within forty yards, one of the war party held up a scalp and others began firing. One of the shots broke Buchanan's leg. Bowie fired back with a double-barreled gun and a pistol and then carried Buchanan over his shoulder back to camp.

The war party took cover behind a hill to the northeast of Bowie's camp. The "famous shot" of Calf Creek came when a chief on horseback appeared, urging his men to charge. Caiaphas K. Ham was the only one holding a loaded gun at the moment. James Bowie directed him to fire. Ham did, breaking the chief's leg and killing his horse.

The war party now circled Bowie's men, finding cover among trees and rocks and especially on the stream bank to the rear of the camp. Rifle and bow and arrow fire from the warriors began to take their toll among the defenders. At one point Bowie's men were driven from the trees and sought shelter in a nearby oak thicket. From there they were able to silence the sniping fire from the stream.

The war party was unable to dislodge Bowie's men, so they set prairie fires with the hope of driving them into the open. This also failed despite the fact that the fires burned through the thicket where Bowie and his men had taken cover. Those among Bowie's men who were still able formed a ring around the wounded and baggage and resolved to make a last stand with knives drawn as long as one was still standing. Meanwhile they fought the fires with blankets and buffalo robes while two servants, Charles and Gonzales, cleared away flammable brush and built breastworks.

At 5:00 A.M. the next morning the war party could be heard moving off to the northeast. At 11:00 A.M. thirteen of the warriors reappeared but then left quickly. Bowie's men raised a flag on a long pole with the hope that it would display their willingness and ability to keep fighting. They remained in their camp for a week until the wounded were able to travel. The party returned to Bexar to the astonishment of the residents, who had already been told by the Comanches that the Bowie brothers and their party all had been killed.

Casualties:

The Bowie party lost one man killed and three wounded. The war party's losses were heavier and more difficult to estimate. James Bowie reported that he and his companions saw twenty-one warriors fall dead. Rezin Bowie described counting forty-eight bloody spots on the ground where dead and wounded had lain. Caiaphas Ham stated the Comanches said the number was fifty-two killed.

Outcome:

There were no real victors in this battle. The Bowies and their companions may be considered victors by the mere fact that most of them managed to survive against great odds. The Native Americans were not exactly defeated although they did fail in their attack with considerable losses. They ended their attack when the cost far exceeded the gains. No one actually found the lost silver mines. If anything, the battle enhanced the fighting legend of James (Jim) Bowie.

Location:

A number of locations have been suggested for the site of this battle. One is Bowie Springs on Celery Creek north of Menard in Menard County. The generally accepted site is off FM 1311 in western McCulloch County twenty to twenty-five miles south of Brady. It is on privately owned land.

Markers:

There are two Texas historical markers describing the Calf Creek fight. One is located on Ranch Road 1311, a half mile south of Calf Creek. The other is one-and-a-half miles southeast of Calf Creek on FM 1311. The descriptions are identical except that one describes the number of the war party as 164 and the other 163. Both markers describe 80 of the warriors as having been killed. There is a Bowie Battleground Monument on FM 1311, sixteen miles southwest of the town of Brady in McCulloch County. Many miles away, in Uvalde County at the intersection of U.S. 83 and SH 127, there is a Texas historical marker which describes "Silver Mine Pass (2 mi. W)," and describes the fight as having taken place in that vicinity. It also mentions the remains of a fortification supposedly built by Jim Bowie and his men. According to this marker the Bowie party's fight was against Comanches. It also praises Bowie's slave "Black Jim Bowie" for leaving the fortification during the battle to bring water to the besieged.

Bowie's Company at the Calf Creek fight:

Rezin P. Bowie
Robert Armstrong
James Bowie
David Buchanan (wounded)
Charles
James Coryell (wounded)
Matthew Doyle* (wounded)
Gonzales
Caiaphas K. Ham
Thomas McCaslin (killed)
Jesse Wallace

*James Bowie's description of the battle, which appeared in *Frontier Times*, does not mention this individual but does list a Mateo Dias. This was probably due to a misinterpretation of a handwritten document.

Velasco
26 June 1832

Opponents:

Texan settlers

    Captain John Austin

        100-150 men

Army of the Republic of Mexico

    Colonel Domingo de Ugartechea

        91-200 men

The Battle of Velasco resulted from friction between the settlers along the Brazos River and Colonel Juan D. Bradburn, the Mexican military commander at Anahuac. Bradburn had taken several Texans, including future Alamo commander William Barret Travis, prisoner. When negotiations to free the prisoners failed, the Texans planned to move against Anahuac.

The force under John Austin and Henry Smith commandeered the schooner *Brazoria*, loaded two cannon and about twenty men aboard, and sailed it down the Brazos River. The rest of the settlers followed on foot along the east bank of the river.

Colonel Domingo de Ugartechea, who had been a cadet in the Spanish Royalist army at the Battle of the Medina, commanded the fort of Velasco on the east side of the Brazos River. When the *Brazoria* arrived Ugartechea denied it permission to pass. The Texan settlers decided to attack Fort Velasco rather than Anahuac.

The fort consisted of a circular wall made of two rows of posts, six feet apart and filled with sand. The fort was 300 feet wide and contained two buildings and a number of tents. A nine-pound cannon was positioned on a high earthen mound in the center.

The settlers were prepared to attack at dawn on June 26, 1832, but an accidental discharge of a Texan's gun just after midnight alerted the fort and the battle was on.

The *Brazoria* traded cannon fire with the fort while the settlers on land moved close enough to be inside the range of the fort's cannon. The two sides fired blindly at one another until after dawn when the Mexican army's ammunition began to run low. Austin demanded and received Ugartechea's surrender.

Casualties:

Seven settlers were killed at Velasco and anywhere from fourteen to twenty-seven wounded. Mexican losses are reported from five killed and sixteen wounded to as high as forty-two killed and seventy wounded. The lesser figure is probably more accurate. A Texan doctor treated the wounded on both sides.

Outcome:

The Texan settlers were the victors in this prelude to the Texas Revolution, but gained very little by it. They allowed the Mexican troops to return to the town of Matamoras with their baggage and side arms via the *Brazoria.* Later the fort was peacefully returned to a different force of the Mexican army.

Location:

The town of Velasco was located sixteen miles south of Angleton and four miles from the Gulf of Mexico. Old Velasco declined after the Civil War. A new Velasco was laid out in 1891. It was incorporated with Freeport in 1957 and is now part of the Brazosport area. The fort is described as having been 150 yards from the seashore near the bank of the Brazos River not far from the present-day U.S. Coast Guard Station. The site is on public land, but some of it has been destroyed by channel improvements.

The Brazoria County Historical Museum and Research Center and the Brazoria County Library can provide information on this battle. (See information under Jones Creek battle.)

Markers:
A Texas historical marker mentioning the Battle of Velasco is located in front of City Hall in Surfside, Texas

Nacogdoches
2 August 1832

Opponents:
Texan settlers
    Captain James W. Bullock
        Approximately 500 men
Army of the Republic of Mexico
    Colonel José de la Piedras
        Approximately 500 men

The Battle of Nacogdoches, like the Battle of Velasco, came about as a result of rising tensions between Texan settlers and Mexican military garrisons in Texas. The underlying cause of this growing tension was the 1830 decree by Mexican President Anastasio Bustamente forbidding further immigration to Texas from the U.S. The direct spark which ignited the Battle of Nacogdoches was the order of Colonel José de las Piedras, military commander at Nacogdoches, to the local citizens to surrender their arms. Piedras feared a repetition of the events at Fort Velasco a month earlier.

The settlers naturally resisted, and citizens from Nacogdoches formed a militia and sent out word to the surrounding communities for help. On August 2, 1832, forces from these communities rallied to the east of Nacogdoches and elected James W. Bullock as commander. An ultimatum of surrender was sent to Piedras by the settlers. He refused and fortified several buildings within the town, including the Stone House, a church, and his own residence, the Red House.

The Old Stone Fort Museum in Nacogdoches
(Photo by Rod Timanus)

The Texans attacked from the east side of town, and Piedras's men advanced to meet them. Reports on what time the battle started vary from 11:00 A.M. to 2:00 P.M. Most of the Texans were driven back by a charge of Mexican cavalry. Approximately a hundred of the settlers began a house-by-house advance through the town, driving the Mexican forces from each building. Piedras pulled back and concentrated his defense at the Red House. A force of Texans advanced from the north side of town and drove off the Mexican cavalry. The fighting continued until nightfall when Piedras and his men managed to evacuate Nacogdoches.

A force of Texans pursued them on the following morning, and a running fight along the Angelina River ensued. Piedras's men began to turn against him, and he finally turned over command to Captain Francisco Medina, who surrendered the Mexican force.

Casualties:

The Texan settlers lost three killed and from four to seven wounded, one of whom died later. The Mexican losses are recorded as from thirty-three to forty-seven killed and from seventeen to forty wounded.

25

Outcome:

The Battle of Nacogdoches ended the Mexican military presence in east Texas. Piedras was taken to San Felipe and paroled to Mexico. James Bowie escorted the Mexican troops to San Antonio de Bexar where they were released. Another result of this battle, along with that of Velasco, is that it may have caused Texans to underestimate Mexican military ability. This notion would prove tragic to many during the Texas Revolution four years later.

Location:

Nacogdoches is the county seat of Nacogdoches County and is located 100 miles north of Beaumont. The Stone House, which played a role in the Gutiérrez-Magee expedition, the Fredonian rebellion, and the Battle of Nacogdoches was torn down in 1902. It was rebuilt with the original stones in 1936 on the campus of Stephen F. Austin State University. It is now called the Stone Fort Museum and is located at College Drive and Griffith Boulevard.

Stone Fort Museum
   PO Box 6075
   Stephen F. Austin State University
   Nacogdoches, Texas 75962-60759
   Tuesday-Saturday 9 A.M.-5 P.M.
   Sunday 1 P.M.-5 P.M.
   Closed Mondays and holidays
   Guided tours are available but require a reservation
   There is no admission fee

Markers:

There is a Texas historical marker commemorating the Battle of Nacogdoches located at the corner of Fredonia and El Camino Real (Main) in Nacogdoches. Another marker is located in Cherokee County seven miles east of Alto on SH 21. It designates the "Site of Linwood" and mentions that the Battle of Nacogdoches ended there.

Chapter Two

The Texas Revolution

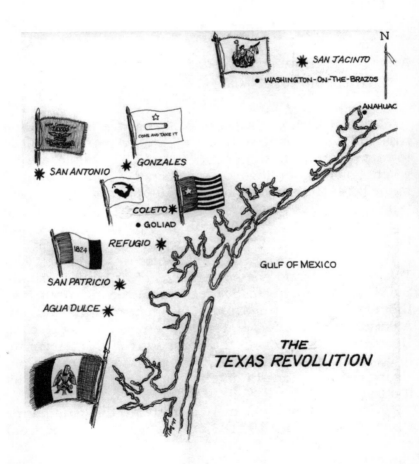

THE
TEXAS REVOLUTION

Gonzales
2 October 1835

Opponents:

Texan settlers

    Colonel John Henry Moore

    Lieutenant Colonel J.W.E. Wallace

        Originally 18 men, whose number may have increased to 140

Army of the Republic of Mexico

    Lieutenant Francisco de Castañeda

        Approximately 100 dragoons

The Battle of Gonzales is recognized as the opening round of the Texas Revolution, and it has earned the little town the title of "Lexington of Texas." The trouble started when Colonel Domingo Ugartechea, then military commander in Texas, sent Lieutenant Francisco de Castañeda from San Antonio de Bexar to Gonzales with 100 dragoons to retrieve a bronze cannon. The cannon had been given to the citizens of Gonzales four years earlier as a deterrent to hostile Indians. With relations between Texan settlers and the government of Antonio Lopez de Santa Anna on a steady decline, Mexican authorities thought it wise to remove this weapon from the settlers. An attempt by one corporal and five enlisted men failed, so Ugartechea dispatched the force under Castañeda to make a stronger demand. Knowing the touchy situation, Ugartechea cautioned Castañeda to avoid armed conflict if possible.

Castañeda and his men arrived at the Guadalupe River on September 29, 1835. They were prevented from crossing the river by eighteen local citizens who later became immortalized as the "Old Eighteen." The eighteen informed Castañeda that he would have to wait on the west side of the river for the return of Andrew Ponton, the alcalde of Gonzales. Castañeda set up camp while the eighteen began to receive reinforcements. Meanwhile the cannon had been buried in a peach orchard to hide it from the Mexican troops.

Word reached the Mexican camp that the Texan force had grown to 140 men with more on the way. Castañeda decided to find a better place to ford the river and moved his camp seven miles upstream.

The Texans crossed the Guadalupe with the controversial cannon which had been dug up and a newly made flag that featured a picture of a cannon in the center and the invitation to "Come and Take It." The Texans followed Castañeda to his new camp and attacked the Mexican force on the morning of October 2. After a brief truce and parley during which Castañeda tried to determine why he was being attacked, the force resumed fighting. Finally, Castañeda prudently removed his men back toward Bexar.

If there was any "famous shot" of the Battle of Gonzales it was surely the first (and possibly only) time the "Come and Take It" cannon fired. It irrevocably set the course toward revolution.

Casualties:

The Mexican force lost one man killed. The Texans suffered no casualties.

Outcome:

This battle, which was little more than a skirmish, was a victory for the Texan settlers in that they retained possession of their cannon and sent the Mexican force back toward San Antonio de Bexar. After this incident there was no turning back from revolution for the Texans.

Location:

The town of Gonzales is located in Gonzales County on U.S. 183, about seventy miles east of San Antonio. For a battle as small as Gonzales was there is plenty in and around the town to help remember it.

The Gonzales Pioneer Village-Living History Center is located one-half mile north of Gonzales on U.S. 183. The Village features ten historic buildings from different periods of nineteenth-century Texas. During special events held several times a year, reenactors in period costume perform demonstrations of pioneer life. Most notable of these is the "Come and Take It Days" held the first weekend in October. The Battle of Gonzales is reenacted during this festival.

In the town of Gonzales itself is the small but impressive Gonzales Memorial Museum. This museum commemorates the "Immortal 32" men from the town who rode to the aid of the Alamo and lost their lives there. An amphitheater behind the museum displays a plaque honoring the "Old Eighteen." The showpiece of the museum is a small iron cannon purported to be the original "Come and Take It" cannon. This cannon was unearthed in 1936 (the Texas Centennial) after a major flood. Some historians, most notably Thomas R. Lindley of Austin, dispute this claim, since the cannon matches none of the contemporary physical descriptions of the gun and it appears to be of iron rather than bronze.

Gonzales Memorial Museum
    414 Smith
    Gonzales, TX 78629
    Tuesday - Saturday 10 A.M.-12 P.M., 1-5 P.M.
    Sunday 1-5 P.M.

Gonzales Pioneer Village
    PO Box 431 Gonzales, TX 78629
    210-672-2157
    September-May
    Saturday 10 A.M.-5 P.M.
    Sunday 1-5 P.M.
    June-July-August
    Friday 10 A.M.-4 P.M.
    Saturday 10 A.M.-5 P.M.
    Sunday 1-5 P.M.

Markers:

The town of Gonzales is a historical marker rich environment. There are some eighty-six historical markers in and around Gonzales. At least nine of these are Texas historical markers concerning the Battle of Gonzales. This can cause a little confusion since the markers are spread all over the vicinity of town, yet, with a quick read, they all can convey the idea that they mark the spot where the battle actually took place.

One marker is located on the 200 block of St. Louis Street. It is entitled "First Shot of the Texas Revolution," but it commemorates the alleged spot that the Gonzales cannon was buried when the Mexican army came to claim it. One mile south of Gonzales at the Guadalupe River Bridge are two markers side by side. One is dedicated to "18 Texians" and lists the "Old Eighteen." The other commemorates the "Site of Gonzales Cannon Dispute" and describes it as the site where the Mexican troops demanded the return of the cannon. On the south city limits at a turnout on U.S. 183 a marker describes the "Battle of Gonzales." A marker entitled "Santa Anna Mound" is lo-

31

cated 1.7 miles south of Gonzales on U.S. 183, and it describes the place where the Mexican troops camped from September 29 to October 1. Six miles south of Gonzales on SH 97 is a bronze and granite memorial monument to the "First Shot Texas Revolution." Six and one-half miles southwest of the juncture of SH 97 and 95 is a marker which states that it is on the exact spot of "The First Shot of the Texas Revolution." In the town of Cost, three miles southwest of SH 97 on 95, there is a monument which describes the "Site of the First Shot of the Texas Revolution Near Gonzales." Directly opposite this monument is a small marker describing "The First Shot of the Texas Revolution" as being one-and-one-half miles from the spot. Finally, there is a small monument at the end of a small road one-and-one-half miles from the previous ones, donated by the children of Gonzales, which allegedly marks the exact spot where the first shot was fired.

The "Old Eighteen":

Captain Albert Martin	Almeron Dickerson
Almond Cottle	(Dickinson)
Jacob C. Darst	George W. Davis
Benjamin Fuqua	Ezekiel Williams
John Sowell	Winslow Turner
Valentine Benet	Simeon Bateman
James B. Hinds	Wm. W. Arrington
Charles Mason	Joseph D. Clements
Thomas R. Miller	Gravis Fulcher
Thomas Jackson	

Concepción
28 October 1835

Opponents:

Army of the Republic of Mexico
  Colonel Domingo de Ugartechea
  Lieutenant Colonel José María Mendoza
    275 men
Texan Revolutionary army
  Colonel James Bowie
  Captain James Walker Fannin
    90 men

The Battle of Concepción was the first armed clash during the siege of San Antonio de Bexar, which began in late October of 1835. After the Texan victory in the skirmishing at Gonzales, the Texan army began to grow. Stephen F. Austin was elected commander of this force, and his first action was to move against the Mexican force occupying Bexar. Colonel James Bowie and Captain James W. Fannin were ordered to proceed from the mission San Francisco de la Espada south of Bexar and find a position closer to town. They traveled north on October 27, 1835, as far as the mission Nuestra Señora de la Purisima Concepción and camped along the San Antonio River after a brief skirmish with Mexican scouts.

General Martin Perfecto de Cos, in command of the Mexican army at Bexar, sent Colonel Domingo de Ugartechea out on the following morning with a 275-man force consisting of cavalry, artillery, infantry, and two cannon. At about 8:00 A.M. that morning Mexican scouts surprised one of the Texan pickets in the morning fog. They exchanged gunfire and the fight was on. Mexican cavalry held the west side of the river while the infantry and artillery, under Lieutenant Colonel Mendoza, crossed over and attacked the Texans from below their position. Skirmishing went on for two hours until the fog lifted. Mendoza's force then deployed in a long line to either side of one of their cannon and advanced on the Texans' positions.

Bowie ordered a company commanded by Robert M. Coleman to meet the advance. The Mexican troops charged while grape and cannister from their artillery rattled through the trees above the Texans. They were soon driven back by the Texan rifle fire. Texan sharpshooters concentrated on the artillerymen, forcing them back with the infantry. Mexican officers rallied their men and renewed the attack twice while the Texans inched along the river toward the Mexican position. Finally, the Mexican officers ordered a retreat. As their troops fell back the Texans rushed forward, captured their cannon, and fired a parting shot at them.

Austin and the rest of his army joined Bowie about one-half hour after the fighting had ended. Austin urged pursuing the retreating Mexican force into Bexar itself and continuing the battle there. His officers, however, believing that the town was too well fortified, talked him out of the idea.

Casualties:

The Mexican army lost fourteen killed and thirty-nine wounded. The Texan force lost one killed and one wounded.

Outcome:

Concepción was a heady victory for the Texan Revolutionary army and reinforced in their own minds the false notion of their superiority against Mexican troops. The battle also caused General Cos to adopt a strictly defensive position in the town of Bexar leading to the siege of Bexar.

Location:

The Battle of Concepción took place about a quarter mile west of mission Nuestra Señora de la Purisima Concepción. This site is now part of modern day San Antonio, and the course of the San Antonio River has been altered since the time of the battle. Mission Concepción is part of the National Park Service and can be visited as part of San Antonio's Mission Trail. It is located about three miles south of the Alamo.

Markers:

There is a plaque marking the site of the Battle of Concepción on Theo Avenue in Concepción Park in San Antonio. Fifteen miles west of the town of Andrews in Andrews County there is a Texas historical marker in a roadside park on SH 176. This marker describes the creation of Andrews County and explains that it is named for Richard Andrews, who was killed in the Battle of Concepción.

Lipantitlán #1
4 November 1835

Opponents:

Army of the Republic of Mexico and civilians of San Patricio, Texas

> Captain Nicolás Rodríguez
> > Approximately 90 men

Texan Revolutionary army

> Adjutant Ira J. Westover
> > 60-70 men

In late October 1835, Philip Dimmitt, the commander of the Texan garrison at Goliad, ordered his adjutant Ira Westover to take and destroy the Mexican army's fortification at Lipantitlán, west of San Patricio. Dimmitt wanted Lipantitlán destroyed because of its strategic importance to the Mexican army should they attempt to retake Goliad. Another reason was Dimmitt's desire to lay his hands on Captain Manuel Sabriego, commander of the local rancheros. Sabriego had been paroled by Stephen F. Austin, because of Sabriego's Federalist sympathies, after the

Texans had seized control of Goliad three weeks earlier. Dimmitt became enraged when Sabriego continued to work for and support the Centralist forces after his parole.

Westover left Goliad with thirty-five men but accumulated additional men along his line of march. By the time he reached Lipantitlán he had sixty to seventy men with him. Fort Lipantitlán was an earthen fortification strengthened by wooden fence rails. Only twenty-one to twenty-seven men defended it with two cannon after its commander, Captain Nicolás Rodríguez, marched towards Goliad with the majority of his command.

Rather than storm the fortifications at Lipantitlán, Westover used James O'Riley, an Irish native and citizen of San Patricio whom Westover's men had made a prisoner, to negotiate a surrender of the small Mexican force. O'Riley was successful, and the Texans seized the fort without firing a shot.

After burning some buildings around the fort and attempting to destroy the earthworks, Westover and his men set out back toward Goliad. While they were crossing the Nueces River they were intercepted by Captain Rodríguez and his force, who were returning to Lipantitlán.

Westover posted some of his men on the east bank of the river while about half of his men crossed over and took positions among the trees on the opposite side. Rodríguez's men attacked and attempted to outflank the Texans. The left wing of the Mexican attack was led by ten Irish citizens of San Patricio, among them the alcalde, the judge, and the sheriff of the town. The Texan rifle fire quickly took its toll on the Mexicans. After thirty minutes of fighting, Captain Rodríguez ceased the attack and withdrew.

Casualties:

Rodríguez's force lost twenty-eight to forty-three men killed, wounded, or missing, depending on the source. This number includes the three officials of San Patricio, all of whom were wounded. The Texans suffered one man wounded who lost three fingers of his right hand and suffered a fractured left hand by the same ball.

Outcome:

The capture of Fort Lipantitlán and the defeat of its garrison temporarily cut off the Mexican line of communication between General Cos at San Antonio de Bexar and Matamoras, Mexico. This contributed to Cos's defeat in the Battle of Bexar.

Location:

The Battle of Lipantitlán, sometimes known as the Battle of Nueces Crossing, took place on the east bank of the Nueces River about three miles north of San Patricio in present-day San Patricio County.

Markers:

Fort Lipantitlán was located on the west bank of the Nueces River along the Atascosito Road. Today its site is part of the Lipantitlán State Historic Site. This five-acre site is located at FM 624 and FM 70 in Nueces County. There is a stone marker to indicate the site, but there is no reconstruction of the fort.

Grass Fight
26 November 1835

Opponents:

Texan Revolutionary army

    Colonel James Bowie

    Colonel William H. Jack

        Approximately 140 men

Army of the Republic of Mexico

        Approximately 100 men

The Grass Fight was another minor engagement during the siege of Bexar. Texan scouts were on the lookout for Colonel Domingo Ugartechea, who had been sent to Laredo by General Cos to lead reinforcements to Bexar. On November 26, 1835, Texan scout Erastus (Deaf) Smith reported that a Mexican column and supply team had been spotted approaching Bexar. The assumption was that it was Ugartechea, and a rumor circulated that the supply train carried silver to pay the Mexican troops in Bexar.

Stephen Austin had left the field in order to solicit aid for Texas in the U.S. Colonel Edward Burleson had been elected by the men to replace him. Burleson ordered James Bowie with forty cavalrymen to delay the supply train while one hundred infantry under the command of Colonel William H. Jack followed. Bowie met and attacked the Mexican force of about fifty men approximately one mile southwest of town. Both sides fought on foot using streambeds for cover. General Cos dispatched fifty of his infantrymen and one cannon to support the cavalrymen. When Jack arrived on the scene he and his men became pinned down in a cross fire between the Mexican cavalry and infantry. The Mexican troops were driven back by Texas cavalry under James Swisher but kept up a stubborn fight. Their cavalry rallied and counterattacked three times followed by one counterattack by the infantry. The

Texans were preparing to meet this attack in hand-to-hand combat when Swisher's men turned the tide by closing in on the Mexican cannon. The Mexican troops disengaged from the battle and pulled back into Bexar.

Casualties:

The Texans suffered four wounded in this fight. The Mexicans lost three men killed and fourteen wounded. Some sources put the Mexican losses as high as forty to fifty.

Outcome:

The Texans enjoyed another minor victory, but they did not seize any silver treasure. The forty pack animals they captured were carrying fodder for the Mexican army's animals, hence the name Grass Fight.

Location:

The Grass Fight is believed to have taken place near the junction of the Alazán, Apache, and San Pedro Creeks just southwest of San Antonio de Bexar. Today the site is within modern San Antonio near the San Antonio stockyards.

SAN ANTONIO DE BÉXAR

SAN PEDRO CREEK

THE ALAMO

N

SAN ANTONIO RIVER

GRASS FIGHT

CONCEPCIÓN

Markers:

A Texas historical marker commemorating the Grass Fight stands in front of Lanier High School on South Brazos Street just off West Durango Street in San Antonio. This marker also mentions the Battle of Bexar.

Bexar

5-9 December 1835

Opponents:

Texan Revolutionary army

    Edward Burleson

    Colonel Benjamin R. Milam

    Colonel Francis W. Johnson

        Approximately 560 men

Army of the Republic of Mexico (Permanent Battalion of Morales, Presidial Cavalry Corps)

    General Martin Perfecto de Cos

    Colonel Nicholás Condelle

    Colonel Domingo de Ugartechea

        Various counts with the maximum being approximately 1,050 men, only about 600 of whom were effective troops

The Battle of Bexar was the culmination of a siege of San Antonio de Bexar begun in late October 1835. After the Texan victory in the skirmishing at Gonzales, the Texan army began to grow. Stephen F. Austin was elected commander of this force, and his first action was to move against the Mexican forces occupying the town of San Antonio de Bexar and the Alamo mission.

The Texan forces settled down to a very loose siege of the town in the early weeks of November. They fought in a few small engagements and skirmishes with the Mexican forces while trying to lure General Cos out of the fortifications in the town and the Alamo.

As the Texan force increased in number throughout November, at least two plans to attack Bexar were made. These were ultimately decided against by the democratic procedures of the volunteer army. The Texan soldiers also engaged in politics during the siege. When Austin left the field to set up diplomatic ties with the U.S., they elected Edward Burleson as their commander.

Burleson planned for an attack on the town on December 4 but vacillated when it was feared that General Cos had become aware of the plan. Finally, the frustrated Texan troops took matters into their own hands. William Cooke and Ben Milam called for volunteers who would be willing to press the attack with them. Three hundred men stepped forward and Burleson agreed to support the plan with a reserve force.

The battle began in the early morning hours of December 5, with Texan artillery under Colonel James C. Neill shelling the Alamo on the east side of the San Antonio River as a diversion. The assault troops in two divisions under Milam and Francis W. Johnson attacked the town from the north. Burleson remained in overall command directing the reserves and cavalry who patrolled the outskirts of the town. What followed was four days of gruelling street-by-street, house-to-house fighting. The Mexican defenders contested every inch of Bexar, but the Texan invaders pushed ever closer to the fortified plazas in the center of town.

The famous (or infamous) shot in the Battle of Bexar came on December 7 when Ben Milam and Francis Johnson met in the Veramendi house to plan a nighttime advance. As the men walked into the courtyard a single shot rang out, allegedly fired by Felix de la Garza of the Mexican army, and Milam fell dead.

The Texans pressed their attack as the Mexicans fell back. Finally, on the afternoon of December 8, Cos abandoned defenses in the town and consolidated his forces in the Alamo mission. Morale among the Mexican troops collapsed when four of their cavalry companies failed to join them in the Alamo. Cos's position became untenable, and on the morning of December 9 he surrendered to Burleson.

Casualties:

The Texan forces suffered four dead and another fourteen wounded, although some sources say that their casualties were as high as thirty to thirty-five. The Mexican army probably suffered a hundred and fifty casualties, despite exaggerated numbers in a variety of sources.

Outcome:

The Battle of Bexar ousted the Mexican army from Texas. Burleson paroled Cos and his men since the Texans had neither enough men to guard nor provisions to feed prisoners. This battle also marked the end of the first stage of the Texas Revolution, and hostilities ceased until the Mexican army's return in late February of 1836.

Location:

The Battle of Bexar took place in and around the town of San Antonio de Bexar, which grew into the modern city of San Antonio. It is difficult to visualize the battle in the modern surroundings. Visits to the José Antonio Navarro house at 228 S. Laredo Street or the Spanish Governor's Palace at 105 Plaza de Armas can help evoke a sense of period. Of course the Alamo's Long Barracks Museum contains information and displays pertaining to the battle. The Daughters of the Republic of Texas Library at the Alamo is probably the best local starting place for information on the battle.

Markers:

There is a Texas historical marker on U.S. highway 87, three miles east of San Antonio, which marks the "Site of the Camp of Stephen F. Austin October 20-26 1835." Also the "Cos House" in the La Villita Historical District of San Antonio is identified as the place where General Cos signed the surrender terms after the battle. The Texas historical marker at South Brazos and West Durango Streets concerning the Grass Fight also mentions the Battle of Bexar.

San Patricio

27 February 1836

Opponents:

Army of the Republic of Mexico

    General José Cosme Urrea

        Approximately 400 men

Independent force of the Texan Revolutionary army

    Colonel Francis White Johnson

        Approximately 34-52 men

The Battle of San Patricio was the result of an ill-conceived plan by certain members of the Texan army to strike into Mexico. The target of the plan was the town of Matamoras on the Rio Grande, and an expedition was mounted under Colonel Francis W. Johnson and Doctor James Grant. The idea was a controversial one. On the surface it was intended to rally liberals who opposed the Centralist government of Santa Anna to the Texan cause. Below the surface Johnson and Grant sought to protect vested interests in the Matamoras area, and their men had hopes of certain plunder. Whatever the reason for the expedition, it succeeded in drawing off much-needed men and supplies from the Texan army. Despite opposition from General Sam Houston and others, the expedition got under way with the consent of the Texan governing council.

The expedition never reached its goal of Matamoras, turning, instead, into a horse roundup in the vicinity of the town of San Patricio. Johnson and Grant split their force, with Johnson taking some of the men and the horses to San Patricio while Grant ranged further south in search of more horses.

Johnson continued to divide his men. One group went to a ranch south of town with the horses. Johnson and the rest divided into four groups and camped in separate locations within San Patricio.

General Urrea had marched north from Matamoras. He caught Johnson and his men completely by surprise at about 3:00 A.M. on February 27, 1836. It could not have been much of a "battle." Johnson and four others managed to escape. The rest were killed or captured.

Casualties:

The generally accepted numbers for casualties among the Texans at San Patricio are eight killed and eighteen taken prisoner in the town, and four killed and eight taken prisoner with the horse herd. Six are believed to have escaped.

Outcome:

San Patricio was an easy victory for the Mexican army. Valuable men and supplies which could have been used elsewhere by the Texan army were wasted.

Location:

Modern San Patricio is located in San Patricio County approximately ten miles up the Nueces River from Corpus Christi.

Markers:

There is a Texas historical marker on the school grounds in modern San Patricio describing the founding of the original town "San Patricio de Hibernia." The marker also briefly mentions the battle.

Agua Dulce Creek
2 March 1836

Opponents:

Army of the Republic of Mexico

　　General José Cosme Urrea

　　　　Various estimates as to the number of men

Independent force of the Texan Revolutionary army

　　Dr. James Grant

　　　　Various estimates, 22-46 men

After Johnson and Grant split their force, Johnson went to San Patricio and Grant and his men ranged south in search of more horses. General Urrea decimated Johnson's force on February 27. He learned of Grant's mission while at San Patricio and turned his sights toward him.

On the morning of March 2, 1836, Grant led his men and the horses they had rounded up back toward San Patricio. Grant and two others rode well ahead of the rest. General Urrea had set an ambush for the group. He allowed Grant and his two companions to pass between two stands of trees. When Grant's main body of men and horses arrived Urrea's troops struck. The Mexican force charged from the trees and quickly surrounded Grant's men. Grant and Reuben Brown, who were riding ahead, rode back to the fight. Their other companion, Placido Benavides, was sent to warn Colonel Fannin at Goliad. When the horse herd that Grant's men had been leading broke through the Mexican lines Grant and Brown went with them. They were chased by the Mexican cavalry for six or seven miles before being ridden down. Grant was killed and Brown taken prisoner, thus ending the "battle" of Agua Dulce.

Casualties:

The casualties at Agua Dulce vary as do the number of participants. The generally accepted numbers for the

Texan losses are twelve killed, six taken prisoner, and six who escaped. Five of the escapees went from the frying pan into the fire when they rejoined Fannin's command at Goliad. General Urrea variously reported forty-one to forty-three Texans killed. The Mexican losses are not reported. Brown stated that Dr. Grant killed a Mexican soldier after the soldier had lanced Brown through the arm. If there were any others killed or wounded, the losses must have been minimal.

Outcome:

The outcome of this fight was much like that of San Patricio. It was a victory for the Mexican army and deprived the Texan army of much-needed men. It also made a gift of many horses to the Mexican army.

Location:

There are a number of locations reported for the site of the battle at Agua Dulce. Some sources say that it took place twenty-six miles south of San Patricio. Others place it five miles north of the town of Banquet. The Texas historical marker which describes the battle states that it is three and a quarter miles northwest of the marker which itself is two miles east of Agua Dulce.

Markers:

A Texas historical marker commemorating the Battle of Agua Dulce is located on SH 44 two miles east of Agua Dulce in Nueces County.

Alamo
6 March 1836

Opponents:

Army of the Republic of Mexico

Generalissimo Antonio Lopez de Santa Anna

Approximately 2,200-2,400 men

Texan Revolutionary army

Lieutenant Colonel William Barret Travis

Approximately 250 men

The Alamo is the most famous of all Texas battles. It has been the source of countless books, films, myths, and legends. It is the one we are even admonished to "remember." The scene for the Alamo battle was set in the aftermath of the Battle of Bexar. General Cos and his men were driven out of Texas and the danger of invasion by Mexico was not very immediate. Boredom and lack of money and provisions began to take their toll on the men who were left to garrison San Antonio de Bexar. Many left to return to their homes and families, and the garrison dropped to as few as eighty men in early 1836. The Texan commander at Bexar, Colonel James Clinton Neill, recognized the danger and began to send off a series of messages requesting reinforcements, money, and supplies. His request for aid had a limited effect, and several small groups of reinforcements joined his command during January and February of 1836. Most notable among these groups was a regular cavalry unit under Lieutenant Colonel William Barret Travis, a volunteer group under James Bowie, and a volunteer group of recent arrivals to Texas that included David Crockett. One large force was approaching San Antonio at this time, but, unfortunately for

Antonio Lopez de Santa Anna
(Courtesy of the Institute of Texan Cultures, San Antonio, Texas)

the Texans, it was the Mexican army of General Antonio Lopez de Santa Anna, bent on avenging the defeat of Cos and reclaiming Texas.

In mid-February Neill left San Antonio to personally press his requests for supplies and money. He left Travis, the highest ranking regular officer, in charge in his absence. On February 23 the vanguard of the Mexican force along with Santa Anna himself appeared outside of San Antonio. The Texans abandoned all hope of defending the town and concentrated all their men and artillery in the Alamo.

The Alamo, originally the mission San Antonio de Valero, was questionable as a defensive position. Construction on it had begun in 1724 with the cornerstone of the church laid in 1744. It was a sprawling complex of walls and buildings covering approximately three acres, much too great an area for the Texans to defend with the amount of men they had.

Santa Anna settled down to a siege that lasted the next thirteen days while the rest of his forces arrived. It was a loosely conducted siege in which messengers were able to leave and enter the fort. They carried pleas from Travis for aid. Like Neill before him, he was moderately successful. At least one but probably two reinforcements arrived from the town of Gonzales, seventy miles to the east. Messages also came in. One from Travis's friend Robert McAlpin Williamson, commanding officer of the Texas Ranging companies, urged Travis to hold out since 300 men were on their way and 300 more were expected. Other groups were on their way, most notably one under Captain Juan Nepomuceno Seguin, who had been sent out of the Alamo to rally aid, and another under Colonel Neill, who was returning to his command. Before any more help could arrive, however, Santa Anna made his move. On March 4 he convened a meeting of his officers and decided to assault the Alamo.

In the predawn hours of Sunday, March 6, four columns of Mexican infantry supported by cavalry and a reserve assaulted the walls of the Alamo. Three columns under General Cos, Colonel Francisco Duque, and Colonel José Maria Romero attacked the northern section of the mission, catching the north wall in a pincer movement. The fourth column under Colonel Juan Morales attacked from the south, probably as a diversion. The cavalry under General Joaquín Ramirez y Sesma patrolled the perimeter to prevent the escape of the defenders. The reserves along with Santa Anna were stationed to the northeast.

The Texan defenders had spent the night before shoring up their defenses. Undoubtedly they were tired and worn out from thirteen days of siege. They were not completely caught by surprise, however. One of the Mexican columns, caught up in the excitement of the moment, began to cheer for Santa Anna. The Alamo garrison's adjutant John Baugh sounded the alarm, and the Texans were alerted.

The defenders opened up with cannon and small arms fire before the Mexicans could place their scaling ladders. Briefly, the attack columns faltered but quickly rallied.

The sheer force of numbers became too much for the thinly spread defenders, and the Mexican troops gained a foothold on both the north wall and south corner of the Alamo. Travis had been one of the first Texan casualties at the north wall. He had been struck in the head by gunfire at one of the artillery positions in the opening moments of the battle. With Travis dead and the Mexican soldiers pouring over the walls from two different directions, the loosely organized defense quickly fell apart. Defenders abandoned their positions on the walls. Some jumped inside the walls and sought cover in the Alamo's buildings. Others jumped outside the walls. Some of these were cut down by the Mexican cavalry. At least one group made a last stand in a ditch outside the walls. Another small group of six or seven was captured near the San Antonio River and executed.

According to Santa Anna the battle ended by 8:00 A.M. Santa Anna entered the fort with his entourage to inspect the battle's aftermath. While in the fort he ordered the execution of a handful of defenders who had been taken prisoner. The only defenders who were spared were Joe, Travis's slave, and possibly Brigido Guerrero, who is supposed to have convinced Santa Anna's men that he had been a prisoner of the Texans. Approximately twenty women and children inside the Alamo survived the battle. Several children may have been killed. It is also likely that a number of unidentified slaves survived. At least one female slave was reported by Joe to have been killed in the battle. If any of those defenders who jumped the walls managed to escape, it has not been recorded by history.

The Texan bodies were burned in three large pyres in an area known as the Alameda just south of the Alamo. Many of the bodies of the Mexican soldiers were buried. Others were simply thrown into the San Antonio River which, along with the burning bodies of the Texans, caused an especially ghastly scene for the residents of Bexar.

Casualties:

The casualties listed for both sides of the Alamo battle are as legendary as the battle itself. Depending on the telling the Mexican losses are listed as from 70 to 2,000 and the Texan losses as from 183 to 600. Actually the Mexican army probably suffered 200 to 300 casualties during the battle with many of the wounded dying later due to Santa Anna's failure to provide a medical unit with his force. Although the Texan losses are usually given as 183 to 189, new research by Thomas R. Lindley of Austin indicates that as many as 250 to 260 probably died defending the Alamo.

Outcome:

The Alamo was a costly victory for the Mexican army. It put San Antonio back into the hands of the Mexican government for a while. It taught the rebellious Texans a sobering lesson in the realities of war and placed their forces on the defensive.

Location:

At the time of the battle the Alamo was separated from the town of San Antonio de Bexar by the San Antonio River. The west wall of the mission was approximately one-half mile to the east of the center of town. The city of San Antonio has grown up and around the site of the Alamo. The present-day Alamo is right in the heart of modern San Antonio located on Alamo Plaza between Houston and Crockett Streets.

Today the Alamo is the most popular tourist site in Texas. It is maintained as a shrine and museum by the Daughters of the Republic of Texas. The site is very different from the Alamo of 1836. The former church is still the main building of the complex. It serves as the shrine to the defenders of the Alamo. There are displays of artifacts of a number of defenders, flags representing the states and nations of their origin, and bronze plaques with the names of those currently recognized to have been defenders of the Alamo. A park area opens up behind the church.

Slightly north and west of the church entrance is the Long Barracks Museum where a short film of the battle is shown, as well as artifacts, weapons, and displays explaining the Alamo's transition from mission to fortress to shrine. A separate Sales Museum building serves as a souvenir and book shop as well as displaying weapons, tools, and photographs relating to the history of the Alamo and Texas. The Daughters of the Republic Library is located on the grounds and is the best starting place for research on the Alamo and other aspects of San Antonio and Texas history. Alamo Hall, located behind the Library, is a former San Antonio city fire station. It now serves as a meeting hall.

There are two major points of confusion to people visiting the Alamo for the first time. Many people are disappointed when they see the Alamo in the center of San Antonio when they expected to see an intact fortress out on the Texas plains. Also, many are confused by the physical makeup of the site. The original church building is the main structure of the Alamo today as it was in 1836. At the time of the battle, however, the main area of the Alamo opened out in front of the church. Today, the Alamo's grounds open out behind the church/shrine and are enclosed by walls built in the 1930s. Many visitors mistakenly believe that these walls were the ones defended by Travis and his men, despite a number of dioramas, relief maps, and diagrams which explain the configuration of the original fort. A newly published Alamo brochure does much to clear up this confusion by providing a diagram which overlays the configuration of the original mission with that of the modern grounds. Also the Wall of History alongside the Sales Museum has very detailed illustrations of the evolution of the property through the years.

San Antonio's Alamo Street runs directly through what was the Alamo's plaza. A row of stores takes the place of the fort's west wall. The position on the north wall where Travis died is now inside the U.S. post office. A flower bed now takes the place of the buildings which comprised the south wall.

For those interested in getting a feeling for what the original Alamo was like, a trip along San Antonio's Mission Trail is recommended. This trail stretches for about ten miles south of the Alamo and leads to four other Spanish missions: Nuestra Señora de la Purisima Concepción; San José y San Miguel de Aguayo; San Juan de Capistrano; and San Francisco de la Espada. All give an indication of what the Mission San Antonio de Valero and the fortress Alamo must have been like. For those whose interest in the Alamo was inspired by Hollywood films, a side trip to Brackettville, Texas, is also recommended. Brackettville lies approximately 130 miles west of San Antonio. The Shahan ranch there served as the location for John Wayne's 1960 film *The Alamo*. A one-third scale reproduction of the original fortress was constructed for this film and was later used in a number of other Alamo related films and westerns. Much of the structure, with many renovations, still stands today, as well as a small movie set version of San Antonio de Bexar. It is a good site for those who wish to get a feeling for what the Alamo was like without the distractions of a modern city. It is a working movie location, and visitors may actually get to see a movie, TV show, or video being filmed.

Back in San Antonio and in walking distance from the Alamo are two sites which are a must for anyone interested in the Battle of the Alamo. One is the San Antonio Imax Theater in the Rivercenter Mall about half a block southeast of the Alamo. It shows the film *Alamo-The Price of Freedom* six times daily. The film is exciting, if a bit hokey at times, and it is mercifully short (45 minutes). In addition to the film there are museum-quality displays of weapons, uniforms, photos, and illustrations of the Alamo. There is also a very interesting model of San Antonio de Bexar as it appeared in 1836, done by George Nelson. The other site is the Texas Adventure Theater across Alamo Street from the Alamo. It is an "Encountarium Special Effects Theater" and presents a unique 24-minute story of the Alamo as told by 3-D ghostly figures of the main Texan participants. Artwork by Joe Musso of California enhances the story. This theater also displays a fabulous diorama by Tom Feely of New Jersey. It depicts Crockett's last stand in the area in front of the Alamo Chapel. One of Tom's dioramas is also on display in the Alamo's Sales Museum.

The Alamo
> PO Box 2599
> San Antonio, TX 78299
> 210-225-1391
> 210-229 1343 FAX
> Winter hours
> Monday-Saturday: 9A.M.-5:30 P.M.
> Sunday: 10A.M.-5:30 P.M.
> Summer hours
> Monday-Saturday: 9A.M.-6:30 P.M.
> Sunday: 10 A.M.-6:30 P.M.
> Open daily except Christmas Eve and Christmas Day.

Daughters of the Republic Library at the Alamo
> PO Box 1401
> San Antonio, TX 78295-1401
> 210-225-1071
> 210-212-8514 FAX
> Monday-Saturday 9 A.M.-5 P.M.
> Closed holidays

Alamo Village
> PO Box 528
> Brackettville, TX 78832
> 830-563-2580
> 830-563-9226 FAX
> Seven miles north of Brackettville on FM 674
> Brackettville is approximately 130 miles west of San
>   Antonio
> Daily 9 A.M.-5 P.M. (Labor Day to Memorial Day)
> 9 A.M.-6 P.M. (Memorial Day to Labor Day)
> Admission summer: $7 adults, $4 children under 12,
>   free for children under 5

Admission winter: $6 adults, $3 children under 12, free for children under 5

San Antonio Imax Theater
  Rivercenter Mall
  849 Commerce Street
  San Antonio, TX 78205
  210-225-6517
  210-225-4629
  Showings of *Alamo–The Price of Freedom*:
  9 A.M., 11 A.M., 1 P.M., 2 P.M., 4 P.M., 6 P.M.
  Admission: adults $6.95, seniors $6.50, children ages 3-11 $4.75
  (Although the address is Commerce Street, it is easier to enter the theater from Crockett Street, especially when walking from the Alamo.)

Texas Adventure Theater
  307 Alamo Plaza
  San Antonio, TX 78205
  210-227-8224
  210-227-9855 FAX
  210-227-0388 groups, private parties, or tours
  Admission: adults $6.50, children $4.50, seniors and military with I.D. $5.90

Markers:

There are a number of Texas historical markers commemorating the Alamo. One is located on Alamo Plaza and the other in the Alamo itself. Two new markers have been put up recently. One is dedicated to Adina de Zavala, one of the modern day saviors of the Alamo. It is located between Alamo Plaza and Alamo Street, just opposite the present-day Long Barracks Museum. The other describes the Alamo's Low Barracks and main entrance. It stands in the vicinity of the flower planter, the area formerly occupied by the Low Barracks. In 1939 a sixty-foot-high Alamo Cenotaph designed by Pompeo Coppini was erected on Alamo Plaza to commemorate the men who sacrificed

Alamo Cenotaph
designed by Pompeo Coppini

their lives in defense of the Alamo. The San Fernando Cathedral at 115 Main Plaza, San Antonio, displays a sarcophagus which is said to contain remains of Alamo defenders.

Some of the leading Mexican and Texan officers at the Alamo:

Mexican

Generals

Antonio Lopez de Santa Anna
Juan Valentine Amador
Juan José Andrade
Manuel Fernandez Castrillón
Martin Perfecto de Cos
Joaquín Ramirez y Sesma

Colonels

Juan Nepomuceno Almonte
Augustin Amat
José Batres
Juan Bringas
Francisco Duque
José Miñon
Esteban Mora
Juan Morales
José Maria Romero
Mariano Salas

Texans

Lieutenant Colonel William Barret Travis
Colonel James Bowie
Majors

Green B. Jameson
Robert Evans

Captains

William C. M. Baker
John J. Baugh
Samuel B. Blair
William Blazeby
William R. Carey
Almeron Dickinson
William B. Harrison
Albert Martin
Juan N. Seguin (not present during the battle)

Refugio
12-15 March 1836

Opponents:

Texan Revolutionary army

    Lieutenant Colonel William Ward

    Captain Amon B. King

        Approximately 148 men

Army of the Republic of Mexico

    General José Cosme Urrea

        Approximately 1,500 men

Captain Amon B. King had been sent by Colonel Fannin from Goliad to evacuate families in the town of Refugio. The town was directly in the path of General Urrea's army and had already been invaded by a force of Mexican ranchers who were acting as an advance unit of Urrea's force.

Instead of simply rounding up the families and leaving, King, with his twenty-eight men, went after the ranchers. The ranchers, however, proved to be too much for King's force. He was forced to retreat with the families to the mission Nuestra Señora de la Refugio. He managed to get a messenger to Fannin, informing him of their plight.

Fannin responded by sending Lieutenant Colonel William Ward and 120 men, mostly Ward's own Georgia battalion, to relieve King. Ward arrived at the mission on March 13, and instead of evacuating the mission, he and King began to bicker about who was actually in command and what action to take. King finally took his own men, and some of Ward's, and went after the Mexican ranchers. After King and his force left, General Urrea arrived with his main force and trapped Ward and his men in the mission. King attempted to return to the mission, but he and his men became trapped along the Mission River. Both Texan forces held out against Mexican attacks until the following day when Ward, following orders from Fannin, escaped with most of his men. He attempted to rendezvous with Fannin at the town of Victoria. King's men also attempted to escape during the night but were captured the next day. King and most of his men were executed. Ward's men made it as far as Dimmitt's Landing where they surrendered to Urrea's troops on March 21. He and most of his men were executed six days later in the Goliad Massacre.

Casualties:

It is estimated that Urrea lost approximately a hundred men killed and fifty wounded in the Battle of Refugio. Most of King's men taken prisoner were executed. Mexican Colonel Juan José Holsinger spared six Refugio colonists and two native born Germans. Most of Ward's men taken prisoner were also executed, except for a handful spared to work as boatwrights for the Mexican army at Victoria.

Outcome:

The Mexican army continued to enjoy the momentum of victory after victory. The Texan army continued to carve itself up piece by piece and obligingly serve itself to General Urrea. Ward's failure to return to Fannin's force at Goliad set the stage for the next and most tragic stage of the revolution for the Texan army.

Location:

Refugio is the county seat of Refugio County. It is located on U.S. 77 about thirty miles north of Corpus Christi. The Refugio mission no longer exists. A recent excavation at the site has been filled in. The land is owned by the Catholic Church but it is open to the public.

Markers:

A Texas historical marker commemorating "The Urrea Oaks" marks the traditional spot of General Urrea's camp in 1836. The marker also mentions King, Ward, and the Battle of Refugio. It is located on U.S. 77 one-half mile south of Refugio. There were two monuments erected to King and his men in 1936. One is in the town of Refugio, the other is in the Mount Calvary Catholic Cemetery near Refugio.

Coleto

19-20 March 1836

Opponents:

Army of the Republic of Mexico

    General José Cosme Urrea

        Approximately 700-1,000 men

Texan Revolutionary army

    Colonel James Walker Fannin

        Approximately 300 men

On March 13 or 14, 1836, Colonel Fannin at Goliad received a communication from General Sam Houston ordering him to blow up Fort Defiance (the presidio La Bahia) and remove all of his men and any artillery which could be transported to Guadalupe Victoria. Fannin did not immediately obey Houston's order. He was still awaiting the return of Ward and King from Refugio. He was also waiting for carts and oxen to be delivered to him from Guadalupe Victoria since King had taken all of Fannin's teams and wagons with him. Meanwhile, General Urrea, reinforced by the Jiménez and San Luis battalions fresh from their victory at the Alamo, moved steadily toward Fort Defiance.

By March 17 Fannin had learned of Ward's and King's fate, and his scouts had made contact with advance units of the Mexican army. Still, he did not get underway until the morning of March 19, taking nine cannon and about 1,000 muskets with him, but not enough food and water. Much valuable time was wasted on this retreat in dealing with broken wagons, dragging a lost cannon out of the San Antonio River, and allowing the hungry oxen to graze. The Mexican cavalry overtook the Texans by early afternoon.

Fannin attempted to reach the cover of trees along Coleto Creek and then the closer Perdido Creek by forming his force into a moving square. The breakdown of an ammunition wagon forced him to take a position in the open, on low ground covered by high grass, and with no water. He managed to form his men into a defensible square, three ranks deep with cannon at the corners, before General Urrea could bring up his troops for an attack.

Urrea launched a four-sided attack on Fannin's square involving infantry, dismounted dragoons, cavalry, and artillery. The Texans, armed with a number of rifles or muskets, each put up a spirited defense which impressed even Urrea. The battle lasted until sunset with the Texans repelling three Mexican charges.

During the night Fannin and his officers weighed their options. They had little food or ammunition and not enough water to cool the cannon or to care for the wounded (one of whom was Fannin). The idea of abandoning the wounded was considered, but, to the credit of the men, the unwounded unanimously voted against this. The Texans entrenched their position during the night using baggage, carts, and even dead animals as a barricade.

On the following morning, March 20, Fannin and his officers decided that they would not be able to sustain another attack. After the Mexican artillery lobbed a few shells at their position, the Texans sought surrender terms. There has been great controversy regarding these terms, mostly involving whether or not Fannin fully understood them and whether or not he clearly conveyed the terms to his men. At any rate he surrendered, placing the fate of his men totally in the hands of the Mexican government with only Urrea's pledge to intercede on their behalf with Santa Anna.

Fannin and his men were taken back to Goliad and held in the presidio La Bahia while Urrea continued on toward Guadalupe Victoria. Santa Anna ignored Urrea's recommendations of mercy for the Goliad prisoners. On March 27, 1836, Colonel José Nicolas de la Portilla, in accordance with Santa Anna's orders, executed Fannin and most of his men, including Ward and his Georgia battalion. A handful of doctors and medical assistants were spared to treat the Mexican wounded. Others managed to escape the slaughter.

Casualties:

The record of Mexican casualties at Coleto varies widely. One source describes approximately fifty killed and one hundred forty wounded. The Texans lost seven killed and sixty wounded during the battle. The majority of the prisoners were executed, a few were spared, and approximately twenty-eight escaped.

Outcome:

The Battle of Coleto was a significant victory of the Mexican army over the amateur Texan army. It virtually wiped out whatever was left of the Texan army, forcing Sam Houston to rebuild the force from scratch. It also instilled great overconfidence in Santa Anna, which proved disastrous to him later on. The mass executions hurt the Mexican cause and filled the Texans with a thirst for revenge.

Location:

The site of the Battle of Coleto is maintained by the Texas Parks and Wildlife Department as the Fannin Battleground State Park. It is near the town of Fannin in Goliad County about nine miles east of Goliad on FM 2506 and about one-half mile south of U.S. 59. The park consists of a circular drive surrounding a stone obelisk dedicated to Fannin and his men. A small room in an octagonal building has three interpretive panels with photos and descriptions of the events leading up to the disaster, the battle itself, and the Goliad massacre. Picnic tables are available in covered areas above and alongside this building.

Our Lady of Mount Loreto Chapel at the Presidio La Bahia in Goliad

A reconstructed Presidio La Bahia can be visited in Goliad. The fort was restored in the 1960s, making it the only fully restored Spanish fort in the U.S. On display are many artifacts, weapons, artwork, and photos concerning the site's role in the Texas Revolution as well as its earlier history. Mass is still celebrated in Our Lady of Loreto Chapel, the site's oldest building. It was here that the Texan prisoners from the Battle at Coleto were taken after their surrender.

Fannin Battleground State Historical Park
    PO Box 66
    Fannin, TX 77960
    8 A.M.-5 P.M. daily
    $2.00 admission fee per car (honor system)
    (A small sign at the entrance warns visitors to be careful of the snakes.)

Presidio La Bahia
    PO Box 57
    Goliad, TX 77963
    1-512-645-3752
    daily
    $3.00 adults, $1.00 children

Markers:

A short distance to the southeast of the Presidio is the Fannin Memorial Monument marking the place where the bones of the massacre victims were discovered in 1932. The bones were reinterred in the Mount Calvary Catholic Cemetery in Refugio two years later. Fannin Plaza at Market and Franklin Streets in Goliad features a memorial to Fannin and his men that was

Stone obelisk at the site of the Battle of Coleto, near the town of Fannin

65

erected in 1885. A Texas historical marker commemorating the "Battle of Coleto and Goliad Massacre" is located in Goliad State Park on the west side of U.S. 183, one mile south of Goliad. Another marker describing the "Graves of Colonel J. W. Fannin and His Men" is located in an enclosure near the Fannin Memorial Monument off Spur 71. A Texas historical marker in Brazoria County on FM 521 indicates the "Site of Home of James Walker Fannin."

Survivors of the Goliad executions:

Thomas G. Allen	John C. Holliday
William Brenan	William L. Hunter
Zachariah S. Brooks	Milton Irish
Samuel T. Brown	David J. Jones
Bennett Butler	Thomas Kemp
Dillard Cooper	William Mason
Neill John Devenny	Daniel Martindale
John Crittenden Duval	Daniel Murphy
Herman Ehrenberg	John Rees
William Haddon	Charles B. Shain
Isaac D. Hamilton	Augustus W. Sharpe
Nathaniel Hazen	Wilson Simpson
Joseph W. Hicks	Sidney Van Bibber
Benjamin H. Holland	John Williams

Spared at the Goliad executions:

Dr. Joseph H. Bernard	George Pittuck
Dr. Joseph E. Field	William Rosenbury
Andrew Michael Boyle	William Scurlock
Francisco Garcia	Charles Smith
Peter Griffin	Joseph H. Spohn
Benjamin H. Hughes	John George Andrew Vose
James Hughes	Alvin E. White
Abel Morgan	Ulrich Wuthrich

San Jacinto
21 April 1836

Opponents:

Texan Revolutionary army
General Sam Houston
Approximately 740-900 men
Army of the Republic of Mexico
Generalissimo Antonio Lopez de Santa Anna
Approximately 1,200-1,250 men

Sam Houston gained fame in Texas by winning one battle—the big one at San Jacinto. [From an original oil painting by William Henry Huddle] (Courtesy of the Texas State Library and Archives Commission)

Since word of the Alamo's fall had reached Sam Houston at Gonzales on March 13, 1836, the Texan army had been in retreat. Sam Houston pulled back before Santa Anna's army while gaining recruits until his force numbered almost 1,300 men. Once word of Fannin's defeat and the massacre of his men reached the Texans, a near panic set in, launching the great "Runaway Scrape." Many of the Texan volunteers left the army to care for their families. The Texan army, the Texan government, and civilians all reeled eastward before the Mexican army.

Meanwhile, Santa Anna pursued the fleeing Texans east with three separate forces: General Antonio Gaona toward the northeast, General Urrea from the south, and Santa Anna in the center.

Houston's retreat had taken him as far as Harrisburg by April 19, and from there along the Buffalo Bayou toward the San Jacinto River. On the following morning advance units of the Mexican army made contact with the Texans. Houston's army set up camp with the Buffalo Bayou at its back and with the San Jacinto River on its left. On April 20 a cavalry unit under Colonel Sidney Sherman fought a skirmish with Mexican infantry and came close to bringing on a full-scale battle. By nightfall the Texans found themselves in camp with Santa Anna and his force camped three quarters of a mile away. The Mexican army had marshland, Peggy's Lake, and the San Jacinto River to its rear.

On the morning of April 21, Cos arrived reinforcing the Mexican camp with 540 men and swelling their ranks to more than 1,200. Houston's camp was beset by uncertainty. The men were eager for a fight but they were already outnumbered, and they had no way of knowing if more Mexican reinforcements were following Cos. Houston ordered the scout Erastus (Deaf) Smith to destroy Vince's Bridge which led to their position, thus removing the route of reinforcements (or retreat) for both armies. He then set up his force into a battle formation but still waited. He polled some of his officers during a council of war as to whether the Texans should attack or wait for an attack. The majority favored waiting.

While the Texans debated their next move, the Mexican camp was lulled into complacency. The soldiers lounged behind a breastworks of baggage, saddles, and equipment; Santa Anna retired to his tent, and no one posted any sentries.

In the Texan camp Houston finally made a decision. Despite the opinions of his officers he decided to attack. The Texans started to move toward the Mexican camp at 3:30 to 4:00 P.M. The Second Regiment under Colonel Sidney Sherman was on the Texans' far left. Next to it was the First Regiment under Colonel Edward Burleson. On the far right the cavalry was led by Mirabeau Bonapart Lamar. One day earlier Lamar had been a private and had shown such daring in the skirmish of the 20th that he was immediately given command of the cavalry. Lieutenant Colonel Henry Millard commanded the Regular troops alongside the cavalry. The Inspector General of the Texan

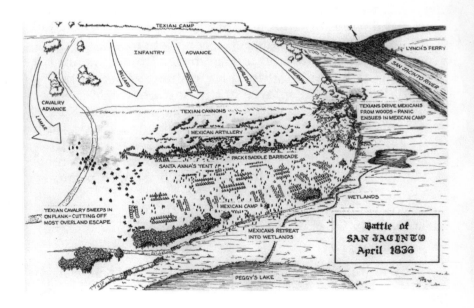

army commanded the artillery in the center, taking the place of Colonel Neill, who had been severely wounded in the skirmishing on the previous day. When the Texans reached a ridge line approximately halfway to the Mexican camp the three fifers and one drummer of the force broke into the tune "Will You Come to the Bower I Have Shaded For You."

The Mexicans in camp finally began to realize that they were under attack, but they were still slow to respond. Houston halted his men long enough for one volley of rifle fire and then they charged with the cries of "Remember the Alamo!" "Remember Goliad!"

The battle lasted for about eighteen minutes. Sherman's regiment on the left pushed the Mexican companies he encountered back behind the breastworks toward his right. The ensuing confusion prevented the Mexican troops from forming into battle formation. General Fernando Castrillón, a veteran of the assault on the Alamo, unsuccessfully attempted to rally a counterattack. He directed the fire of the Mexican cannon, and when his artillerymen were driven back he faced the Texans alone. He was cut down on the breastworks.

The Mexican force suffered a complete rout, and those who tried to surrender found no mercy from the enraged Texans. The killing continued for an hour with a brutality which rivaled that displayed at the Battle of the Medina or during the Goliad executions. Even Sam Houston could not bring his men under control. Santa Anna rode from the field when all appeared to be lost. On the following day a Texan search party brought him into camp. No one realized who he was until other Mexican prisoners began to exclaim "El Presidente!" when they saw him. He was brought before a wounded Sam Houston who spared him despite the wishes of many of the Texans.

Casualties:

The Mexican army lost 630 killed and 730 taken prisoner according to Houston's official report. Only 9 Texans were killed or died from wounds later. Approximately 30 were wounded, including Sam Houston who suffered a painful wound to his ankle.

Outcome:

San Jacinto was a stunning victory for the Texan army. Almost every member of the Mexican force was either killed or captured, including its commander-in-chief. It was a small battle, but it is recognized as one of the most decisive in the world based on its results. Santa Anna was held a virtual hostage by the Texans until their independence was secured. He only returned to Mexico a year later by way of Washington D.C. Texas became an independent republic. Its annexation to the U.S. ten years later led to the Mexican-American War. In the aftermath of this conflict, approximately one-third of the territory of the present-day United States transferred from Mexico to the U.S.

Location:

The San Jacinto battlefield is maintained today as the San Jacinto Battleground State Historical Park by the Texas Parks and Wildlife Department. Like the Alamo it is one of the best and most "visitor friendly" battleground sites in Texas. The centerpiece of the 1,000-acre park is the 570-foot San Jacinto Monument, the top of which is capped by a Lone Star which itself is 34 feet tall and weighs 220 tons. Observation windows at the top offer a panoramic view for miles. The whole obelisk is mirrored in a reflecting pond 1,750 feet long and 200 feet wide. The base of the monument houses the San Jacinto Museum of History, featuring exhibits from the early conquest of Mexico by Spain through Texas of the nineteenth century. It is decorated with eight engraved panels which depict the history of Texas. Also in the base of the monument is the Jesse H. Jones Theater for Texas Studies which shows *Texas Forever!! The Battle of San Jacinto*. This 35-minute multi-image presentation tells the story of the Texas Revolution and the Battle of San Jacinto.

(Photo by Kelly Groneman)

As many as twenty interpretive markers are located throughout the park, identifying spots such as the sites of the Mexican and Texan camps, the spot where Sam Houston was wounded, the spot where Santa Anna was brought before Houston, etc. These spots were identified in 1894 by surviving veterans of the battle and were marked with metal pipes. In 1912 the Daughters of the Republic of Texas had granite markers made up to replace the pipes.

The park is also home to the battleship *Texas* (BB35), the only surviving U.S. warship which served in both world wars. The park offers picnic sites, fishing, and bird watching. Reservations can be made for docking large boats.

San Jacinto is located in Harris County twenty-two miles east of Houston. It is off SH 134 between SH 225 and I-10E.

San Jacinto State Historic Park
   3523 Highway 134
   La Porte, TX 77571
   1-281-479-2431 or 2411
   8 A.M.-9 P.M. daily
   Admission free

San Jacinto Museum of History
   3800 Park Road 1836
   La Porte, TX 77571
   1-281-479-2421
   9 A.M.-6 P.M. daily
   Admission free
   Observation Deck Elevator
   $2.50 adults; $2.00 seniors; $1.00 children
   Texas Forever!! Shown hourly
   $3.50 adults; $3.00 seniors; $2.00 children

For further information call:1-800-792-1112 or use the web site:
   http://www.tpwd.state.tx.us

Markers:

There are a number of Texas historical markers concerning the Battle of San Jacinto. There are six in the vicinity of the San Jacinto Park Cemetery, all with the same description of the "Battle of San Jacinto." There is another in San Jacinto Park on SH 134 with a slightly different description. Near the battleship *Texas* is a marker "1 mi. NE to Site of Lynch's Ferry" that explains the role of Lynch's Ferry in the battle. Across Buffalo Bayou on Zavala Point is a marker "Site of the Home of Lorenzo de Zavala." Zavala was vice-president of the Republic of Texas, and his home served as a hospital for the wounded of San Jacinto. Another marker three miles east of Channel View at Market Street and De Zavala Road is dedicated to "Lorenzo de Zavala (1788-1836)," and it also mentions his home as being used as a hospital after the battle.

**One of the twenty interpretive markers at the
San Jacinto State Historic Park**

Texans killed in the Battle of San Jacinto:

1st Lieutenant	John C. Hale
2nd Lieutenant	George A. Lamb
1st Sergeant	Thomas P. Fowl
2nd Sergeant	A. R. Stevens
Doctor	William Motley
Private	Lemuel Blakely
Private	John Tom
Private	B. R. Brigham

Mexican officers killed in the Battle of San Jacinto:

Brigadier General	Manuel F. Castrillón
Colonels	José Batres

	Antonio Treviño
	Agustin Peralta
	José Avensa
	Estaban Mora
Lieutenant Colonels	Marcial Aguirre
	Dionisio Cos
	Santiago Luelmo
	Cirilio Larambe
	Mariano Olazabal
	Manuel Valdez
	Francisco Aguada
	Miguel Velasquez
Captains	Nestos Guzman
	Benito Rodríquez
	Ignacio Berra
	Ramon Herrera
	Alonzo Gonzales
	Antonio Frias
	Juan Manjoira
	Ramon Rocha
Lieutenants	Jos, Maria Puelles
	Luis Vallejo
	Trinidad Santiesteban
	Juan Santa-Cruz
	Pedro Gonzales
	Antonio Castro
	José Sousa
	Ignacio Brasail
	Antonio Navarro
	Francisco Molino
Second Lieutenants	Joaquín Pavalta
	Basilio Espira
	Juan Montano
	José Maria Torrices
	Victoriano Martinez
	Secundino Rosas

The Texas Revolution is of special interest to reenactors. Each year the San Antonio Living History Association and other organizations preform reenactments of a number of battles. Among these are: Concepción, the siege of Bexar, the beginning of the siege of the Alamo, the fall of the Alamo, and San Jacinto. A moving ceremony is conducted in front of the Alamo at dawn on the morning of March 6. Visitors to Texas Revolution battle sites are encouraged to time their trips to coincide with these reenactments.

San Antonio Living History Association
    3938 Heritage Hill Dr.
    San Antonio, TX 78247

Chapter Three
The Republic of Texas

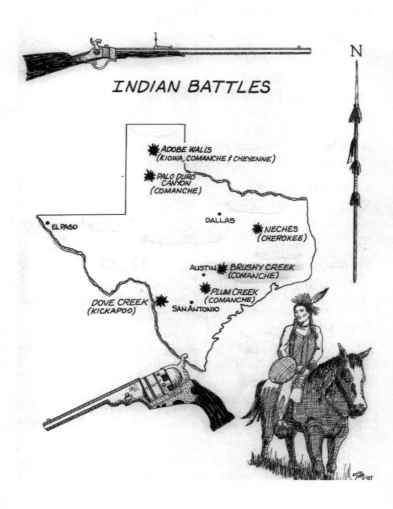

INDIAN BATTLES

N

ADOBE WALLS
(KIOWA, COMANCHE & CHEYENNE)

PALO DURO
CANYON
(COMANCHE)

EL PASO

DALLAS

NECHES
(CHEROKEE)

AUSTIN BRUSHY CREEK
(COMANCHE)

PLUM CREEK
(COMANCHE)

DOVE CREEK
(KICKAPOO)

SAN ANTONIO

Knobs

10 October 1837

Opponents:

Army of the Republic of Texas

    Lieutenant A.B. Van Benthusen

        18 men

Native Americans

        150-250 men

On October 18, 1837, Lieutenant A.B. Van Benthusen led eighteen members of the Army of the Republic of Texas against a much larger group of Native Americans. The outnumbered Texans were beaten and forced to leave their dead on the field when they retreated.

Casualties:

Lieutenant Van Benthusen's force lost ten men killed. It is estimated that the Indians lost approximately fifty men.

Outcome:

This fight had no results other than giving the Texans a sobering reminder of the realities of frontier warfare.

Location:

This fight took place about two miles north of the present-day town of Decatur on the old Meridian Highway in Wise County.

Markers:

There is a Texas historical marker describing the "Battle of the Knobs" on U.S. 287, two miles northwest of the town of Decatur in Wise County.

Stone Houses
10 November 1837

Opponents:

Texas Rangers

    Lieutenant A.B. Van Benthusen

        18 men

Kichai tribe

        150-180 men

    In October of 1837 a company of Texas Rangers unsuccessfully attempted to overtake a party of Kichai warriors in retaliation for a raid on Fort Smith and also to recover stolen horses. After a falling out with the Ranger Captain, Lieutenant Van Benthusen and seventeen others broke off from their company and continued after the warriors on their own. On November 3, they found and killed a Kichai guide who was with a group of Cherokees and Delawares.

    One week later the Rangers encountered the Kichais. The Cherokees and Delawares who had accompanied the Rangers tried to negotiate a peace until one of the Rangers brutally killed one of the Kichais, ostensibly over nothing more than a plug of chewing tobacco. The warriors attacked and soon had the Rangers trapped in a ravine. The Kichais were unable to dislodge the Rangers and resorted to setting a prairie fire to drive them out. Eight Rangers managed to escape under the cover of smoke by running through the Kichais' positions and into the woods. The humbled surviving Rangers returned home over two weeks later with neither their horses nor equipment.

Casualties:

    The Rangers lost four men killed during the fight and six more killed during their escape. The Kichais lost at least two men, one of whom was a chief. Other sources indicate that as many as fifty warriors may have been killed.

Outcome:
This battle had no result other than increasing the Kichais' hatred toward Texan settlers.

Location:
The battle of Stone Houses took place in Archer County about ten miles south of present-day Windthorst.

Markers:
A Texas historical marker indicating the site of "The Stone Houses" and mentioning the battle stands on FM 61 ten miles south of Windthorst in Archer County.

Battle Creek (Surveyor's Fight)
8 October 1838

Opponents:
Kickapoo, Tehuacana, Ionie, Waco, and Caddo buffalo hunters
    Approximately 300 men
Texan civilian surveyors
    J. Neal (Neil)
    Euclid M. Cox
    Approximately 27 men

In the fall of 1838 a group of surveyors traveled to an area which is now southwestern Navarro County. The area was a rich buffalo hunting range for a number of Native American tribes. The surveying party encountered a number of Indian bands as they traveled. At one camp the party shared a stream with fifty Kickapoos. The Indians warned the surveyors that they would be attacked by a band of Ionies. The surveyors were not overly worried about this information and went about their work.

On October 8, 1838, they were fired upon by a group of forty Indians who were hidden in a ravine. Before the surveyors could reach the cover of some woods they were surrounded. They managed to fight their way to two ravines which afforded them some cover.

J. Neal was named leader of the group, probably after the fight started. Euclid M. Cox succeeded him after Neal was wounded. Cox was killed after taking cover behind a lone cottonwood tree at their position and exchanging shots with and hitting a number of Indian snipers.

The Indians attempted several charges but were repulsed each time. Between 11 and 12 o'clock that night the surviving surveyors placed the wounded on their two surviving horses and made for the cover of a nearby woods. The bright full moon gave an advantage to the Indians, who formed a half circle around the group and decimated them with gunfire. Only seven of the surveyors survived. Six made it to the woods. One held back in the ravine and slipped away while the Indians closed in on the others. Three of those who escaped into the woods reached another Kickapoo camp and received aid from the tribe after they convinced them that they had been fighting other Indians. One surveyor, who had been left behind in the woods due to his broken leg, crawled twenty-five miles to safety after splinting the leg himself. A group of fifty men from Old Franklin returned later and buried the unidentified remains of the surveyors beneath the lone cottonwood on the battlefield.

Casualties:

The surveyors lost eighteen killed and four wounded. There are no figures on the Indian casualties, but it is estimated that they suffered twice as many killed and wounded as the surveyors did.

Outcome:

The fight probably did nothing more than to stave off, for a time, the inevitable encroachment of white settlers into this area of Texas.

Location:

The Battle Creek fight took place east of Battle Creek in what is now Navarro County.

Markers:

There is a Texas historical marker identifying the "Battle Creek Burial Ground," one mile west of Dawson on SH 31.

Settlers/Indian Battle
16 January 1839

Opponents:

Settlers from the town of Bucksnort and Bryant Station

Benjamin Bryant

Ethan Stroud

48 men

Possibly the Anadarko tribe

Chief José María

60-70 men

On January 1, 1839, a group of women and children settlers were killed by Indians in what is known as the Morgan Massacre. Nine days later this same war party attacked Fort Marlin where they were fought to a standstill by Garrett Menifee and his son Thomas, who killed seven and wounded several other warriors. In a Texas version of Marathon, Menifee's slave, Hinchey, ran twenty-five miles for help. A group of settlers assembled at Bryant's Station under the command of Benjamin Bryant. They pursued the Indians and caught up with them at Morgan's Point on January 16.

Chief José María initiated the fight with a "famous shot," when he calmly took aim with a rifle and cut the coat sleeve of one of his pursuers. The settlers attacked, driving José María and his men into a dry ravine. Ethan Stroud took over the command of the settlers after Bryant was wounded in the initial attack. The Indians attempted to retreat down the ravine but were flanked by some of the settlers and driven back.

At this point the settlers' undisciplined attack began to disintegrate with the men acting on their own with no organization or control. José María took advantage of the situation by leading a counterattack. Stroud ordered the settlers to fall back to reorganize, but the maneuver quickly became a rout with the Indians in hot pursuit. Some of the settlers who escaped did so by only the narrowest of margins, riding double after being picked up by others.

Casualties:

The settlers lost ten killed and five wounded, including Bryant. José María's men suffered about the same amount of casualties. José María was one of the wounded.

Outcome:

The Indians were the victors in this encounter. Texas patrols were authorized by the government later that year, and violent encounters with Native Americans in this area gradually ceased. José María visited Bryant at Bryant's Station years later where they made peace with one another.

Location:

This fight took place south of Perry and north of Marlin in present-day Falls County.

Markers:

A Texas historical marker identifying an "Indian Battlefield" stands on SH 6, four-and-a-half miles north of Marlin in Falls County. The marker identifies Chief José María as the leader of the Indians involved in this fight.

Brushy Creek
ca. 25 February 1839

Opponents:

Texas Rangers and militia

   General Edward Burleson

   Captain Jacob Burleson

   Captain Jesse Billingsley

     85 men

Comanche warriors

     100-300 men

The Battle of Brushy Creek came about as the result of an unprovoked raid by Texas Rangers under John H. Moore upon a Comanche camp approximately fifty miles northwest of present-day Austin. The raid took place on February 15, 1839, after the camp was reported by Lipan Apaches who joined the Rangers in the fight. The badly outnumbered Rangers and Apaches were driven back, and the Comanches broke off the fight after suffering eighty to a hundred casualties.

The Comanches retaliated on February 24 when they attacked the Coleman and Robertson homesteads north of Bastrop. Mrs. Coleman and her fourteen-year-old son Albert were killed, and the Comanches made off with five-year-old Tommy Coleman and seven black slaves from the Robertson place.

A small group of Rangers followed the raiding party but were too small in number to attack. They were joined by a combined force of about fifty-two men from Well's Fort and Fort Wilbarger under Captain Jacob Burleson.

Burleson led a group of fourteen men ahead to prevent the Comanches from reaching the cover of a thicket. When he dismounted and ordered the others to do so, only two of the men obeyed. The others, reluctant to give up their horses in the face of such a large group of Comanches, rode back to their main force. Burleson and the others, Winslow Turner and Samuel Highsmith, attempted to follow, and Burleson was killed while helping Turner untie his horse. Turner and Highsmith made it back to the main force. After they had pulled back several miles they were joined by Jacob's brother, General Edward Burleson.

Edward Burleson
(Courtesy of the Texas State Library and Archives Commission)

General Burleson sent a party to reconnoiter the Comanches. They reported that their enemy held a strong position on a plateau overlooking Brushy Creek. Burleson devised a plan in which he would lead a company of men and Captain Billingsley another, and they would catch the Comanches in a two-sided attack. The assault got under way as planned, but the Comanches' position proved to be too favorable for defense, and the Ranger companies were unable to cross the open, unprotected areas below the Comanches' guns. The Rangers could only take cover and snipe back and forth with the warriors until nightfall.

The battle ended the following dawn when the Rangers attacked and found the Comanches had slipped away during the night. They left behind much of their equipment and a badly wounded slave. Billingsley attempted to pursue the party but gave up when the Comanches broke up and scattered.

Casualties:

The wounded slave reported that the Comanches had lost about thirty dead and wounded. The Rangers lost four men killed.

Outcome:

There were no real victors in this encounter. The Comanches got away with their captives and eluded the Rangers. The only result of Brushy Creek was that it added further fuel to the hatred between the Comanche tribes and Texan settlers.

Location:

This battle took place in Williamson County in the vicinity of Brushy, Cottonwood, and Bogey Creeks, a few miles from present-day Taylor.

Markers:

In 1925 a red granite marker was set up to mark the site of the battle. It is on private land 1.4 miles south of Taylor on the west side of Highway 95. In 1993 a Texas historical marker commemorating the "Battle of Brushy Creek" was put up on SH 95, four miles south of Taylor.

Córdova Rebellion Battle
29 March 1839

Opponents:

Texan volunteers

General Edward Burleson

Approximately 80 men

Insurrectionists

Vincente Córdova

Approximately 75 men

Vincente Córdova was a prominent citizen of Nacogdoches, Texas, who had fought in the Battle of Nacogdoches and had supported the Texas Revolution while opposing Texan independence. In 1838 and '39 he became involved in a plot with Mexican officials to incite Indian tribes to wage warfare against Texas.

Córdova and his force of Mexicans, Indians, and blacks were fleeing towards Mexico when they were overtaken by General Burleson and his Texan volunteers near Seguin, Texas. Burleson attacked and his force completely routed the insurrectionists.

Casualties:

The insurrectionists lost eighteen to twenty-five men killed and a number wounded, including Córdova, who escaped. Three or four were taken prisoner and one of the blacks was executed. The Texans suffered many wounded but none killed.

Outcome:

This Texan victory put an end to the plot of allying Indian tribes with Mexico against the Republic of Texas.

Location:

This battle took place on Mill Creek about five miles east of the town of Seguin in Guadalupe County.

Markers:

A Texas historical marker entitled "Battleground Prairie" and describing the Córdova Rebellion battle stands on U.S. 90-A, five miles east of Seguin in Guadalupe County.

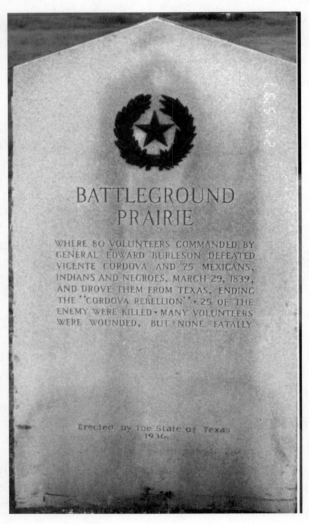

BATTLEGROUND
PRAIRIE

WHERE 80 VOLUNTEERS COMMANDED BY
GENERAL EDWARD BURLESON DEFEATED
VICENTE CORDOVA AND 75 MEXICANS,
INDIANS AND NEGROES, MARCH 29, 1839,
AND DROVE THEM FROM TEXAS, ENDING
THE "CORDOVA REBELLION" • 25 OF THE
ENEMY WERE KILLED • MANY VOLUNTEERS
WERE WOUNDED, BUT NONE FATALLY

Erected by the State of Texas
1936

San Gabriels
17 May 1839

Opponents:

Texas Rangers

Lieutenant James O. Rice

17 men

Insurrectionists

Manuel Flores

20-30 men

In May of 1839 a company of twenty Rangers trailed a party of Mexicans and Indians who had killed four surveyors between San Antonio and Seguin. The party was led by Manuel Flores, who had probably taken part in the Córdova Rebellion battle of March 29. The Rangers caught up with Flores and his men on May 15 between Onion Creek and the Colorado River. Flores's group, which was hidden and waiting to ambush the Rangers in a cedar break, actually taunted the Rangers to attack when they approached. The Rangers hesitated due to their uncertainty of the numbers of enemy they were facing and turned back. Later, angered and probably somewhat ashamed that they had turned back, the Rangers changed course and took up the trail of Flores again.

The command of the Rangers fell to Lieutenant James O. Rice after the Ranger captain's horse became lame and the captain and two other Rangers dropped out. Rice and his men caught up with Flores's party on the North Fork of the San Gabriel River on May 17. The Rangers immediately charged and drove Flores and his men back against a steep bluff. Flores rallied some of his men and led about ten of them in a counterattack. The Texans had taken cover in an oak thicket when William Wallace fired the "famous shot" of San Gabriels and killed Flores. The Mexican and Indian force scattered after Flores's death.

Casualties:

The Rangers suffered no casualties in this fight. Flores's party suffered three men killed including Flores.

Outcome:

The Texans collected a great deal of booty at San Gabriels including almost 160 horses and mules, hundreds of pounds of powder and lead, some Mexican silver, and all of the baggage of Flores and his men. More importantly, the Rangers discovered documents which linked Flores to Córdova and the plot to incite the tribes against Texas. There was also a circular addressed to a number of Indian chiefs, among them Chief Bowles of the Cherokee. This was used as evidence on the part of the Texans to help precipitate the Cherokee War.

Location:

This fight took place on the south bank of the North Fork of the San Gabriel River about nine miles west of present-day Georgetown in Williamson County.

Markers:

A Texas historical marker describing Manuel Flores's death "In This Vicinity" is located on SH 29, four miles east of Liberty Hill and eleven miles west of Georgetown in Williamson County. There is also one dedicated to "James O. Rice" and mentioning the Battle of San Gabriels at the intersection of FM 973 and 1660, eight miles south of Taylor in Williamson County.

Bird Creek
26 May 1839

Opponents:

Texas Rangers

    Captain John Bird

        32-35 men

Comanche and possibly Caddo and Kickapoo buffalo hunters

    Chief Buffalo Hump

        Approximately 300 men

Captain John Bird and his company of Texas Rangers were on patrol for Indians in the vicinity of Little River in May of 1839. On May 25 he and Lieutenant Nathan Brookshire ran off a small party of Comanches who were skinning a buffalo. On the following morning the Comanches returned and stampeded a buffalo herd through the Rangers' camp. The Rangers pursued the Comanches, but the Indians always remained out of range. While they led the Rangers on, individual warriors would break off from the group and smaller groups would return, making the Indians' force ever larger. After pursuing the Comanches for several miles the Rangers gave up. On their return to camp they were surrounded by about forty warriors. Bird led his men to cover in a nearby ravine to escape the hail of arrows being shot at them. The Comanches retired to the top of a hill where 250-300 of them gathered. Brookshire later guessed that some Caddo and Kickapoo warriors rode with the Comanches due to the number of firearms they used.

The Comanches charged and were repulsed several times with heavy losses. Brookshire took over command of the Rangers after Bird was fatally wounded. The Comanche chief, identified as Buffalo Hump, attempted to rally his warriors for another charge, but his men had become exhausted and dispirited. He was able to gather about a dozen men and led them in a final, symbolic charge. It was during this reckless display that one of the two "famous shots" of this battle occurred. James W. Robinett calmly took aim and shot the chief, killing him instantly. Several other warriors died trying to retrieve the chief's body. The other "famous shot" of Bird Creek occurred when Bird was struck in the heart and killed by a single arrow shot from an incredible distance. One source describes the distance as 200 yards. With the death of Buffalo Hump the Battle of Bird Creek ended.

Casualties:

The Rangers lost four men killed, including Bird, and one other who died later. Two others were wounded. Brookshire estimated the Comanches' casualties at thirty to forty killed including their chief and about the same number wounded.

Outcome:

The Rangers were victorious in this battle only to the point of having been able to survive the Comanche attack. Bird Creek was a setback for the Comanches, and afterwards their hostile actions in this area of Texas began to decline.

Location:

This battle took place on what is now called Bird Creek (named after John Bird). The site is located on private land just west of I-35 between Nugent and West Adams Avenues in Temple, Texas.

Information on the Battle of Bird Creek can be found at the Bell County Museum as well as in local libraries.

Bell County Museum
   201 North Main Street
   PO Box 1381
   Belton, TX
   254-933-5243

Markers:

There are two Texas historical markers to the Bird Creek fight in Temple. One, which commemorates the "Bird Creek Indian Battle May 26, 1839" is on Nugent Ave. just north of the battle site. The other, which reads "1/2 mi. N to Bird Creek Battlefield" is located on West Adams Ave. just south of the site.

Texas Rangers killed at Bird Creek:
Captain John Bird
Sergeant William Weaver
Jesse E. Nash
H.M.C. Hall
Thomas Gay

Neches
15-16 July 1839

Opponents:

Army of the Republic of Texas
General Kelsey H. Douglass
General Edward Burleson (Texas Regular army)
General Thomas J. Rusk (Nacogdoches volunteers)
Approximately 500 men

Cherokee Nation, including members of the Delaware and Shawnee tribes
Chief Bowles or Bowl (Chief Duwali)
700-800 men

The Battle of the Neches arose from growing tension between the Republic of Texas and the Cherokee people who were trying to secure land for themselves within Texas. Sam Houston was an adopted member of the tribe and enjoyed a close friendship with the eighty-three-year-old Chief Bowles. Problems developed when Vincente

Córdova opened up a correspondence with Bowles in 1838 while Córdova was attempting to bring Texas back within Mexico. This was enough to convince Texan president Mirabeau Bonapart Lamar that the Cherokees were a major threat to Texas.

Chief Bowles of the Cherokee tribe Sketch by William A. Berry (Courtesy of the Texas State Library and Archives Commission)

Texas officials arranged for negotiations with Chief Bowles in early July 1839 with the intention of convincing the Cherokees to abandon their Texas land peacefully. The Texas government was prepared to reimburse the Cherokees for any property that would have been lost in the move, but not for the land itself.

After two weeks, negotiations broke down completely. On July 15 Chief Bowles and his people abandoned their camp and crossed the Neches River to the west. The Texans under Burleson and Rusk set out in pursuit. When Bowles reached Battle Creek he sent his women and children on ahead and set up a defensive position with his warriors on a high bank of the creek. An advance party of Texans engaged the Cherokees and alerted their position to the main force. Burleson and Rusk split their men and attacked Bowles's position from the front and rear, but by

nightfall they had not succeeded in dislodging the Cherokees. Under the cover of darkness Bowles and his people
again slipped away. The Texans took up their pursuit on
the following morning and found the Cherokees entrenched in a wooded ravine. The Texans launched a
three-pronged attack to drive the Cherokees out into the
open. When this tactic failed the Texans made three
charges and rapid retreats to try to fool the Indians into
chasing them into the open. The Cherokees responded by
sending out a raiding party that almost succeeded in driving off the Texans' horse herd. Finally, a concerted attack
from all four sides forced Bowles's warriors from their
cover. The Cherokees scattered but the last of their
number to leave the field was Chief Bowles, dressed in a
military hat, silk vest, sash, and sword. After his horse
was shot, Bowles, with a severe wound to his thigh, attempted to follow his people on foot until he was shot in
the back. The defiant old chief sat on the ground and
faced his enemies. Captain Robert W. Smith delivered the
"infamous shot" of this battle when he put his pistol to the
back of Chief Bowles's head and killed him. His justifica-
tion was that the twice wounded, eighty-three-year-old
man had not surrendered nor asked for quarter and was
still armed. It was later reported that someone scalped
Chief Bowles and someone else cut a strip of flesh from his
back to use as a razor strop.

Casualties:

The Cherokees lost approximately one hundred killed
and wounded, including their chief. The Texans lost two
killed and thirty wounded.

Outcome:

The Battle of the Neches was a victory for the forces of
the new Republic of Texas. It put an end to the possibility
of the Cherokee nation ever establishing a permanent
home on Texas soil. It virtually ended any impediment to
Anglo-American settlers by Native Americans in eastern

Texas. In achieving this goal Texas may have lost something in the long run.

Location:

The Battle of the Neches was fought just west of Tyler which is located about sixty miles east of Dallas. The fight on the 15th took place in Henderson County, and the one on the 16th in Van Zandt County.

Markers:

There are a number of Texas historical markers concerning the Battle of the Neches in Smith County. There is one on U.S. 69, a quarter mile south of the Sabine River which states, "At this Site was the Camp of the Army of the Republic of Texas." Nine miles northeast of Tyler in a church yard on U.S. 271 another marker commemorates "Scouts of the Texas Army" and mentions the battle with the Cherokees. Another marker is located on U.S. 69, twenty-two miles northwest of Tyler. It reads "On Burleson Lake, 3.5 mi. W of Here Was Last Cherokee War Camp of the Army of the Republic of Texas." In Van Zandt County, thirteen and a half miles west of Tyler on SH 64, a marker identifies the site where Chief Bowles was killed. In Cherokee County, three miles northwest of Alto near Red Lawn, another one shows the site of Chief Bowles's last home but also mentions the battle in which he was killed.

Plum Creek
11-12 August 1840

Opponents:

Army of the Republic of Texas, Texas Rangers, and volunteers

Major General Felix Huston

General Edward Burleson

Captain Mathew Caldwell

Captain Ben McCulloch (Texas Rangers)

Approximately 200 men

Comanche and Kiowa warriors

Approximately 600-1,000 men

On March 19, 1840, a group of Comanche chiefs and warriors along with women and children met with Texan officials in San Antonio. The Comanches were supposed to bring in a number of captives as a show of good faith. The Texans became angered when only one captive was brought and she, Matilda Lockhart, showed obvious signs of abuse including mutilation. The Texans attempted to hold the Indians hostage until more captives were returned, and a fight erupted. In the ensuing violence, which became known as the Council House Fight, many of the Comanche chiefs and warriors and some women and children were killed. In response to this a strong Comanche band numbering almost 1,000 raided into Texas as far as the Gulf Coast. They killed whomever crossed their path, and they sacked the towns of Victoria and Linnville.

As word of the Comanche raid spread, Texans began to assemble to meet the threat. Groups of men under Captain Mathew Caldwell, Captain James Bird, and others joined up at Plum Creek, a tributary of the San Marcos River. On August 12, Major General Felix Huston of the Texas militia arrived and took command of the force. With the arrival of General Burleson and 100 men, including thirteen Tonkawa Indians, Huston was able to plan his strategy and wait for the Comanches.

HORSES WILL BOG DOWN AND STOP IN MARSHY AREA – WARRIORS TRAPPED WITHIN HERD WILL BE SHOT DOWN

PLUM CREEK

TEXAS RANGERS, MILITIA, REGULAR ARMY AND TONKAWA WARRIORS

COMANCHE OUTRIDERS ARE TOO FEW TO MEET TEXAN CHARGE

DETACHMENT MOVES TO CUT OFF MULE TRAIN AND SWING AROUND TO ATTACK HORSE HERD ON LEFT FLANK

HERD OF STOLEN HORSES AND MULES STAMPEDES – MOST WARRIORS ARE SWEPT ALONG IN RUSH

COMANCHE WOMEN AND CHILDREN ABANDON MULE TRAIN CARRYING STOLEN GOODS – WARRIORS BEGIN TO KILL CAPTIVES

Battle of PLUM CREEK Aug. 1840

The Comanches followed the same route back that they had taken into eastern Texas. On August 12 it led them directly toward the waiting Texans. The Indians were in a festive mood, almost giddy with the amount of plunder they had amassed and with the captives they had taken. They drove with them a herd of almost 2,000 horses and mules. They were also laden with dry goods and merchandise they had picked up on the raid. One sight that many Texans recalled was that of a Comanche warrior decked out in a broadcloth dress coat (on backwards), a silk hat, leather boots and gloves, and carrying an open umbrella. The Texans' plan called for them to advance on the Comanches with Caldwell on the left, Burleson on the right, and Major Thomas M. Hardeman bringing up the rear.

The leading group of Comanches took cover in a stand of oak trees as the Texans approached, but the rest of their people were strung out for a quarter mile behind them. The Texans advanced on foot but then remounted and charged. The Comanches fought bravely, but there was no organized defense. Their force broke and scattered after a chief was shot and when the stolen horse and mule herd stampeded. All semblance of cohesion and discipline also broke down in the Texan force much like in the aftermath at San Jacinto. Groups of Texans pursued fleeing groups of Comanches in several running fights, ending the Battle of Plum Creek

Casualties:

The Comanches may have lost forty to eighty killed at Plum Creek. The Texans lost one killed and seven wounded.

Outcome:

The Texans routed the Comanches at Plum Creek but managed to rescue only one captive, Mrs. H.O. Watts of Linnville, who had been found with an arrow in her breast. This was the last major Indian battle in the region and broke the Comanches' power in central Texas.

Location:

The Battle of Plum Creek took place near the present town of Lockhart in Caldwell County. Every June, during the Chisholm Trail Roundup in Lockhart, the battle is re-enacted.

Markers:

A Texas historical marker describing the "Battle of Plum Creek" is located in Lions Club City Park on U.S. 183 in Lockhart.

Village Creek
24 May 1841

Opponents:

Republic of Texas volunteers

General Edward H. Tarrant

70 men

Caddo, Cherokee, and Tonkawa tribes

Approximately 1,000 men

General Edward H. Tarrant raised a company of volunteers in 1841 for punitive raids against various tribes in the Village Creek area of Texas. This was in response to Indian raids against Texan settlements. Previous expeditons against the tribes failed to locate their villages. This time Tarrant and his men captured an Indian who revealed the location of a series of villages along Village Creek, a tributary of the Trinity River.

The Texan force raided and burned one village and sent scouting parties north toward the Trinity River in search of the other villages. The scouting parties traveled north and began to encounter more and stronger Indian war parties. As they began to realize that they were greatly outnumbered and began to suffer casualties, the Texans withdrew from the battlefield.

Casualties:

The Native American tribes suffered about twelve killed and many more wounded. The Texas suffered one man killed and Captain John B. Denton and eight others wounded.

Outcome:

Village Creek was a victory for the Native American forces. However, two years later a treaty opened up this area to settlement, and the tribes were forced on to a reservation.

Location:

This running battle took place along Village Creek, which forms the city limits between Forth Worth and Arlington in Tarrant County. Much of what was the battlefield is now under Lake Arlington, which was created by a dam, just north of I-20 and east of I-820.

Markers:

A Texas historical marker on SH 303 near the Lake Arlington Golf Course is dedicated to "General Edward H. Tarrant" and mentions the Village Creek battle.

Bandera Pass
Spring 1841

Opponents:

Comanche warriors

      Approximately 100 men

Texas Rangers

      Captain John Coffee Hays

         30-40 men

In the spring of 1842 Captain Jack Hays and his Ranger company were on patrol in the Guadalupe Valley. After camping for a night near the town of Bandera, the company entered Bandera Pass from the south. Bandera Pass is a gorge approximately 500 yards long by 125 feet wide. What Hays and his men did not know was that a party of Comanches had entered the pass from the Medina Valley to the north and were waiting in ambush for them.

The Rangers had traveled about one-third of the way through the Pass when the Comanches opened fire with guns and bows and arrows from cover on both sides. The Rangers were thrown into confusion as their horses became almost uncontrollable with the suddenness of the attack. Hays calmly steadied his men and ordered them to dismount.

The Texans returned fire as some of the Comanches charged and the fight soon became hand-to-hand. Sergeant Kit Ackland shot a Comanche chief with a pistol and then the two of them locked with one another in a desperate knife fight. Ackland won the fight, and the Comanches retreated to the north end of the Pass after the death of their chief. The whole battle lasted about one hour.

Casualties:

The Rangers lost five men killed and six wounded. The Comanches carried off their dead and wounded, so the number of their casualties is unknown.

Outcome:

The only result of this fight was that it added to the reputations of a small group of Texas Rangers who would become legendary in Texas history. Among this group were Hays, Ben McCulloch, and William A. A. (Bigfoot) Wallace.

Location:

The site of the Bandera Pass battle is ten miles north of the town of Bandera in Bandera County on U.S. 173. The town of Bandera is about thirty miles northwest of San Antonio.

The Frontier Times Museum as well as local libraries have additional information on the Battle of Bandera Pass.

Frontier Times Museum
   13th St.
   PO Box 1918
   Bandera, TX 78003
   210-796-3864

Markers:

There is a Texas historical marker describing Bandera Pass ten miles north of Bandera on FM 689. There is also one which describes the "Old Texas Ranger Trail" and mentions Hays's battle in Bandera Pass. This marker is located in the town of Bandera on SH 16 across the street from the Bandera Courthouse.

Chapter Four
Incursions-War-Statehood

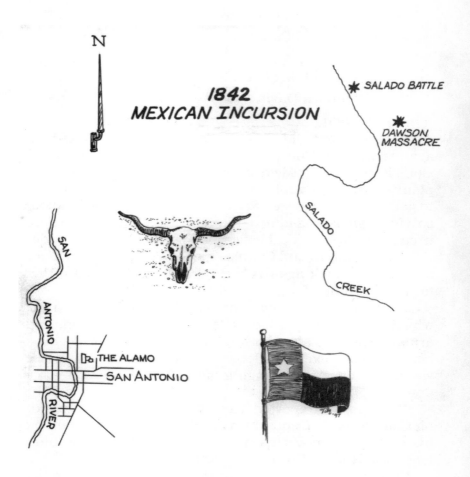

Lipantitlán #2

7 July 1842

Opponents:

Army of the Republic of Mexico (Fourth Infantry, Seventh Cavalry, and auxiliaries)

Colonel Cayetano Montero

Colonel Antonio Canales

457 men

Army of the Republic of Texas

General James Davis

192 men

San Jacinto did not guarantee Texas protection against Mexico. The year 1842 saw a number of incursions into Texas by Mexican military forces. In turn Texas planned retaliatory raids into Mexico. Texan troops began to gather on the Nueces River in late spring. One of Mexico's incursions was aimed at neutralizing this force before it could strike inside Mexico. A Mexican column under Colonels Montero and Canales moved north with plans for a surprise attack against the Texan camp at Lipantitlán for the morning of July 7, 1842.

General James Davis commanded the Texan camp, which was beset by a lack of supplies, ammunition, and arms. There was also a discipline problem. Just five days before the Mexican attack a whole company of Tennessee volunteers deserted, bringing the number of Davis's force down to 192 men.

Texan spies reported the approach of the superior Mexican force to General Davis. He had time to abandon his camp and move his men to a more defensible bluff along the Nueces River some 200 yards away.

Canales and Montero planned to attack the camp before dawn on July 7, but some of their units became lost in the dark. The attack was launched after sunrise when some Texans drifted back into camp to look for forgotten supplies and instead found the Mexican force ready to close in. The Mexicans attacked the empty camp, chasing the few Texans back to their main force.

Canales and Montero reorganized their men and sent a cavalry charge against Davis's position on the bluff. When the cavalry charge was repulsed by Texan gunfire, the infantry and dismounted cavalry were sent in. They too were repulsed, and Canales and Montero resorted to bringing up their single four-pounder cannon to use on the Texans. The "famous shot" of Lipantitlán occurred when a Texan rifleman killed the officer commanding the artillery piece. After the cannon became dismounted and disabled, the Mexican troops began to withdraw from the fight despite evidence that Colonel Canales ordered them into the woods after the Texans. Canales and Montero retained possession of the abandoned Texan camp but abandoned it themselves on the following day, returning to Camargo, Mexico.

Casualties:

The Texans claimed that they only suffered one man wounded. The Mexicans claimed twenty-two Texans were killed. The Mexicans reported four killed, two wounded, and two missing. General Davis estimated that thirty Mexican soldiers were killed or wounded.

Outcome:

Nothing was really gained by this battle by either side, but both sides claimed victory.

Location:

The Texans' camp is said to have been on a small hill in an arc of the Nueces River.

Markers:

A Texas historical marker describing Fort Lipantitlán is located on Fort Lipantitlán Park Road off FM 3088, twenty miles northwest of Corpus Christi and twelve miles northwest of FM 70. The marker mentions the Battle of Lipantitlán but gives the date as "June 7, 1843."

Salado
18 September 1842

Opponents:

Army of the Republic of Mexico

    Brigadier General Adrian Woll

    Juan N. Seguin

        850-1,000 men

Texan volunteers

Texas Rangers

    Captain Mathew Caldwell

    Captain John C. Hays (Texas Rangers)

        Approximately 225 men (14 of whom were Texas Rangers)

Mexico made incursions into Texas, specifically San Antonio, twice in 1842. The first was the Vásquez raid in March. The second came in September when Brigadier General Adrian Woll occupied San Antonio with approximately fifteen hundred men. Texan volunteers from the vicinity of the towns of Gonzales and Seguin marched to San Antonio under the command of Captain Mathew Caldwell to meet the invasion. When they reached the San Antonio area they joined forces with Captain John C. Hays and his Ranger company of fourteen men, who had been forced to pull out of the town with Woll's arrival. Caldwell and Hays did not have enough men to assault the Mexican troops in the town, so they devised a plan to draw the troops out of San Antonio to ground more favorable to the Texans.

On the morning of September 18, 1842, Hays led a group of thirty-eight men (the most the Texans could mount with the number of fresh horses available) to the outskirts of San Antonio to taunt the Mexican force into a pursuit. Caldwell and the rest of the Texan force dug in on a wooded ridge above Salado Creek six to seven miles northeast of San Antonio.

Hays was more successful then he had expected. Woll was already preparing to move against the Texans that morning, and his whole cavalry force was ready to move out when Hays and his men appeared. Hays's force was chased back to the Salado by hundreds of Mexican cavalrymen. They engaged in a running fight all the way back and made it into camp only by the narrowest of margins.

General Woll ordered Captain Francisco Castañeda to attack the Texan position on the Salado. Castañeda responded by calling for help since the Texans held a strong position. Woll mobilized reinforcements which included approximately 400 of his own infantrymen, 40 Cherokee Indians under Vincente Córdova, 160 dragoons, 100 volunteers from San Antonio, and two pieces of artillery.

After Hays and his men rested for awhile, Caldwell sent them out again as skirmishers to induce the Mexicans to attack. In response to Castañeda's continued calls for help, Woll ordered Juan Seguin to attack the Texans' position immediately. Seguin had been a hero of the Texan Revolution but now found himself on the Mexican side after being driven out of Texas by newcomers from the U.S. He led two charges against the Texans but was driven back both times with losses.

General Woll arrived on the scene at about 1:00 P.M. and sent men out to skirmish with a small group of Texans. At around 3:00 P.M. he ordered a full attack and sent Córdova and his Cherokees in a flanking maneuver.

The Mexican troops attacked but were again repulsed by the Texan fire. The flanking attack was also stopped cold, and Córdova himself was killed by a shot from John Lowe.

Woll broke off the fight in the early evening, and during the night he abandoned San Antonio. Pursuing Texans caught up with Woll's force the next day and briefly overran his artillery pieces. The Mexicans counterattacked and regained the guns. Indecision in the Texan camp prevented further action, and Woll's force returned to Mexico.

Juan N. Seguin fought for Texas in 1836 and for Mexico in 1842.
(Courtesy of the Texas State Library and Archives Commission)

Casualties:

General Woll reported twenty-nine of his men killed and fifty-five wounded, but different sources give a variety of casualties with some as high as one hundred four killed and one hundred fifty wounded. The Texan losses are usually given as one or two killed and ten or eleven wounded.

Outcome:

The Battle of the Salado was a victory for the Texans. It ended General Woll's incursion into Texas and prevented him from marching on to Austin.

Location:

The Salado battlefield is located in present-day San Antonio just east of Holbrook Road and north of Rittiman Road in the vicinity of the Mehren House.

Markers:

A Texas historical marker describing "The Battle of the Salado" stands on the east side of Holbrook Road one block north of Rittiman Road.

Dawson Massacre
18 September 1842

Opponents:
Army of the Republic of Mexico
  Colonel Cayetano Montero
  Colonel José María Carrasco
  Colonel Pedro Rangel
    Approximately 500 cavalry
Texan volunteers from Fayette County
  Captain Nicholas Mosby Dawson
    53 men

Captain Nicholas M. Dawson led a company of volunteers from La Grange to San Antonio during General Woll's occupation of the latter. While on the way Dawson received word of Caldwell's impending fight with the Mexican forces. Dawson and his men pressed on alone in an effort to support Caldwell, rather than wait for Captain Jesse Billingsley's company that was trailing about four miles behind.

In the midafternoon of September 18, 1842, while the battle on the Salado Creek was raging, Dawson and his men were trapped about one and a half miles away by Mexican cavalry.

Their posisiton was not a very advantageous one. They were caught out on the prairie with only a small grove of mesquite for cover. When some of the men expressed their concern over the hopelessness of their situation Dawson threatened to shoot the first man who ran or surrendered. Montero advanced with a small patrol under a flag of truce and asked the Texans to surrender. The Texans refused and actually initiated the battle themselves by firing on the main body of Mexican troops after the patrol had returned to their lines.

The Mexican commanders launched a cavalry charge against Dawson's position. It was repulsed by Texan rifle fire after it had closed to within seventy yards of the Texans. The Mexican troops then pulled back out of rifle range and opened up a punishing fire on the Texans with two artillery pieces. Finally the Mexican commanders ordered their men to dismount and attack on foot. This time they slashed their way in with sabers and bayonetts and overwhelmed the outnumbered Texans.

Dawson, who by now was seriously wounded, tried to surrender, but the time for that was long past. He found no mercy. Fifteen of his men, five of whom were wounded, fared better and were taken prisoner. Two others managed to escape. Alsey S. Miller rode toward the Mexican lines showing a white flag. When the Mexican troops continued to fire at him he rode through their lines and escaped. Henry Gonzalvo Woods also tried to surrender. A Mexican officer rode by him and acknowledged him. After the officer rode by, four cavalrymen attacked Woods. Despite being struck over the head with a musket and a sword he wrested a lance from one of the cavalrymen, killed him with it, mounted the man's horse, and got away.

The Texans had fought and lost another valiant yet hopeless battle against the forces of Mexico. One of the Texans especially impressed Colonel Carrasco. He was Griffin, a black slave of the Maverick family. Samuel A. Maverick had been taken prisoner by General Woll when the Mexican army occupied San Antonio. Griffin accompanied Dawson's men in an attempt to gain Maverick's freedom. When the Texans' position was overrun, Griffin used his rifle as a club until it was broken and then fought on with the limb of a mesquite tree until he was killed. Colonel Carrasco described Griffin as "... the Bravest man I have ever seen."

Casualties:

Texan losses at the Dawson massacre were thirty-six killed and fifteen taken prisoner, five of whom were wounded. Of the prisoners nine lived to return to Texas.

Mexican losses are estimated as approximately thirty killed and sixty to seventy wounded.

Outcome:

The Dawson fight was an unfortunate waste of life by both sides. Although the Mexican army was victorious it gained nothing by it. Woll and his men pulled out of San Antonio to return to Mexico on the following day.

Location:

The probable site of the Dawson Massacre is a vacant lot northwest of and adjacent to the intersection of I-35 and Rittiman Road in San Antonio. The lot is private property and is fenced in.

Markers:

A Texas historical marker to the Dawson Massacre stands on the north side of Rittiman Road just west of I-35 in San Antonio just south of the probable battle site. Another monument to the fight stands on the north side of the Austin Highway just west of Holbrook Road in San Antonio. The bodies of Dawson and his men were buried at the site of the battle. In 1848 they were reinterred at La Grange, Texas.

There, on Monument Hill, a tall monument stands in memory of the victims of the Dawson Massacre as well as those Texans executed on the Meir expedition. The Mexican lance that Henry Woods used to effect his escape is on display in the Alamo's Long Barracks Museum.

Walker's Creek (Pinta Trail Crossing)
9 June 1844

Opponents:

Comanche warriors

    Chief Yellow Wolf

        40-200 men

Texas Rangers

    Captain John Coffee Hays

        15 men

Captain Jack Hays and his Ranger company were re-turning to San Antonio from a patrol to the north in early June 1844. They had camped on the Guadalupe River when they spotted a large group of Comanches approaching. The Rangers rode out to investigate as the Comanches took cover in a thicket.

The warriors tried to bait the Rangers into a frontal attack by sending a small group forward. When this failed they rode into the open with their entire force, and the Rangers moved forward to meet them. The Comanches then took cover on the high ground of a nearby hill and continued to taunt the Rangers into an assault.

Rather than be drawn into this trap, Hays led his men around the hill and attacked the Comanches from the rear. A hand-to-hand fight erupted for the top of the hill with the Rangers beating back two counterattacks. The Comanches finally broke off their attack and retreated. The Rangers pursued them for three miles while continuing to fire their revolvers at them.

Casualties:

The Texas Rangers lost one killed and four wounded. Comanche casualties were estimated as anywhere from twenty to fifty killed and wounded, including Chief Yellow Wolf who was killed.

Outcome:

Walker's Creek continued to add to the Texas Ranger's legend and help to sharpen the daring fighting skills with which they would become famous. It is believed that this battle was the first in which revolvers were used. Surely their worth was proven to the Rangers.

Location:

The Battle of Walker's Creek took place along the Pinta Trail northwest of San Antonio. The location is in the vicinity of where I-80 crosses the Guadalupe River.

Markers:

There is a Texas historical marker which describes "The Pinta Trail" on U.S. 290, two miles east of Fredricksburg in Gillespie County, but it does not mention the Walker's Creek battle.

Carricitos
25 April 1846

Opponents:

Army of the Republic of Mexico (cavalry)

    General Anastasio Torrejón

        1,600-2,000 men

U.S. Army (dragoons)

    Captain Seth Thorton

    Captain William J. Hardee

        63 men

When the U.S. annexed Texas in 1845 a conflict arose with Mexico over disputed territory between the Nueces River and the Rio Grande, which both Mexico and Texas had claimed. In a clearly provocative move, U.S. President James K. Polk sent troops under General Zachary Taylor to establish forts along the Rio Grande and occupy the territory. In March of 1846 Taylor arrived at the Rio Grande, and his troops began the construction of Fort Texas. This fort would later be named Fort Brown in memory of Major Jacob Brown, who was killed in the Mexican siege of the fort in May.

On April 25 Taylor dispatched sixty-three dragoons under Captains Seth B. Thorton and William J. Hardee on a scout to determine if Mexican troops had crossed the Rio Grande at a small ranch about twenty-eight miles upriver from the Mexican town of Matamoras. As the dragoons were crossing a large open field near the ranch, they were surrounded by a large Mexican cavalry force under General Anastasio Torrejón. The dragoons tried to break through the Mexican lines but failed. As the Americans attempted to retreat through the heavy brush which surrounded the field, the Mexican troops opened fire on them. Thorton and Hardee were forced to surrender to the vastly stronger force of Torrejón.

Casualties:

The Americans lost eleven killed. The majority of the survivors were taken prisoner, including Thorton and Hardee. A few escaped and made it back to Fort Texas. Thorton and Hardee were later released in a prisoner exchange program.

Outcome:

Carricitos provided President Polk with the excuse for declaring war on Mexico, initiating the Mexican-American War.

Location:

The exact location of the Carricitos fight is not known. It is believed to have taken place about twenty-eight miles upstream from Matamoras and Brownsville, on the Texas side of the river. The site is difficult to determine due to sketchy reports of the fight and also due to the ever changing course of the Rio Grande.

Markers:

There is a Texas historical marker and a small cannon in a roadside park on U.S. 281, twenty-two miles northwest of Brownsville, Texas, which commemorates the Carricitos fight. The marker describes the fight as the "Thornton Skirmish."

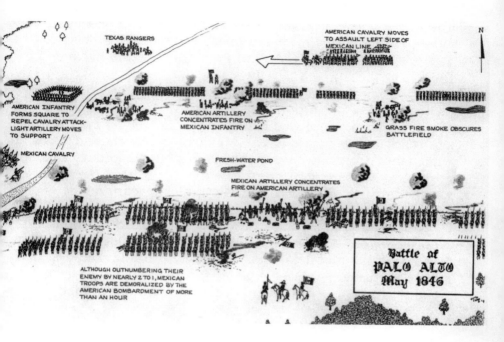

Palo Alto
6 May 1846

Opponents:
Army of the Republic of Mexico

General Mariano Arista

3,400-4,000 men

United States Army

Major General Zachary Taylor

2,200-2,300 men

On April 25, 1846, armed conflict between the United States and Mexico broke out at Rancho de Carricitos, along the Rio Grande. Although war would not be declared until May 13, the first major battle of the war would be fought on May 8 at Palo Alto.

Mexican General Mariano Arista had besieged Fort Texas on the Rio Grande. American General Zachary Tay-

119

lor and his army marched from Fort Polk to the east, where they had gone for supplies, to relieve Fort Texas. Taylor's army found Arista's at Palo Alto midway between the two forts. The Mexican force was deployed across Taylor's line of march on the Matamoras Road. Its flanks were protected by a swamp on the left and a wooded knoll on the right. Taylor deployed his infantry and artillery across the road to the north of the Mexican position, and assigned his dragoons to protect his supply wagons to the rear. Arista opened the battle with an artillery barrage which did little damage. The slow moving cannon balls fired from antiquated field pieces were easily sidestepped by the Americans. Taylor responded by sending Major Samuel Ringgold forward with his newly developed "flying artillery." This mobile artillery could be moved rapidly by specially trained horses to meet the tactical needs of a commander on the battlefield. These more modern pieces

Major General Zachary Taylor
(Courtesy U.S. Army Military History Institute)

opened up on the Mexican line with a variety of exploding shells, causing many casualties.

Arista then sent his 1,000-man force of cavalry to flank the Americans' right side. The U.S. Fifth Regiment moved forward and formed a hollow square to protect Ringgold's artillery. The cavalry charge stalled under the fire of Ringgold's guns. The Mexicans attempted another cavalry charge around the left of the American line directed at their supply train. It too was driven back.

By late in the afternoon a grass fire obscured the battlefield in smoke. Taylor attempted a flanking attack by dragoons on the Mexican left which failed. Arista ordered a final cavalry charge on both sides of the American line. These were again broken up by artillery fire. The battle ended at about 7:00 P.M. when Arista disengaged his troops and moved south.

Casualties:

General Arista listed the Mexican casualties as 102 killed, 129 wounded, and 26 missing. Other accounts put their casualties as high as 500. American losses were four to nine killed, and forty-three to fifty-five wounded. Among those killed was Major Sam Ringgold.

Outcome:

Palo Alto was an indecisive victory for the U.S. Army. It was a victory only to the point that the U.S. sustained less casualties than it inflicted upon its opponent. Arista's force was not defeated, it merely withdrew from the field. One important result of the battle was that Ringgold's "flying artillery" had proven its worth on the battlefield.

Location:

Palo Alto is maintained as the Palo Alto Battlefield National Historic Site by the National Park Service. It is located two miles north of Brownsville in Cameron County at the intersection of SH 511 and 1847. The site has long been on private land, inaccessible to the public. In 1992 a 3,400-acre site was established for the development of a more visitor friendly and historically educational site. Plans are now underway to facilitate this. Information on Palo Alto and other Mexican-American War battles and sites can be obtained from the Palo Alto Battlefield National Historic Site Headquarters in Brownsville, Texas. The headquarters is located on the second floor of the International Bank of Commerce Building and displays interim exhibits and a video on the battle. Brochures and information about Palo Alto as well as other sites can be obtained there. Another good source of information is the nonprofit Palo Alto National Park Committe and its publication the *Palo Alto Dispatch Newsletter.*

Palo Alto Battlefield National Historic Site Headquarters
    1623 Central Blvd.
    Brownsville, TX 78520
    956-541-2785
    Weekdays 8 A.M.-5 P.M.

Palo Alto National Park Committee
    PO Box 3084
    Brownsville, TX 78523-3084

Markers:

A Texas historical marker describing the Battle of Palo Alto is located on FM 1847, five-and-a-half miles north of Brownsville. There are two Texas historical markers on U.S. 77 south of the Kingsville city limits in Kleberg County. One identifies a "Taylor Camp Site, 1846" and mentions the Battle of Palo Alto and the following battle, Resaca de la Palma. The other is an "Honor Roll" naming twelve veterans of the Mexican-American War for whom forts were named in Texas, ten who became commanders in the Civil War, and two who became U.S. Presidents. Another marker on U.S. 77, seven miles south of Sarita in Kenedy County identifies another "Site of General Zachary Taylor's Camp."

Resaca de la Palma
9 May 1846

Opponents:

United States Army

    Major General Zachary Taylor

        2,100-2,200 men

Army of the Republic of Mexico

    General Mariano Arista

        3,100-3,700 men

After retiring from Palo Alto, General Arista moved his forces south and took up a defensive position at Resaca de la Palma, a 200 foot wide, 3 to 4 foot deep dry channel of the Rio Grande, protected by heavy chaparral. Taylor followed with his army but took time to fortify his supply train first. Arista once again deployed his forces across the Matamoras Road, which crossed the Resaca via a bridge, with his artillery in the center, his infantry on both sides of the road, and his cavalry to the rear.

An advance unit of Taylor's army first made contact with the Mexican force. Arista's artillery opened up on them and killed six men. Taylor divided his infantry and placed them on either side of the road with his dragoons to the rear. The flying artillery was sent down the road directly at the center of the Mexican line. The U.S. gunners just managed to turn back a charge by the Mexican lancers which almost overran their position. When pressure from the Mexican infantry forced the flying artillery back, Taylor sent his dragoons forward in an effort to capture the Mexican artillery. Captain Charles May led the charge across the bridge and forced the Mexican artillerymen to abandon their guns. However, May and his men overran the position, allowing the Mexican artillerymen to return and open fire on the dragoons. The Mexican infantry then began to close in, driving the American dragoons back. Taylor finally sent his infantry forward with the order

"Take those guns and by God keep them!" The Americans fought hand-to-hand against the Mexican soldiers in the thick chaparral. Arista, much like Santa Anna at San Jacinto, had been in his tent to the rear during most of the battle. When he eventually arrived at the front the battle was almost over. Arista himself led his lancers in one last futile charge but was unable to break the American attack. Most of his force was spread out through the chaparral and were unable to organize into battle formation. The battle became a rout when the Mexican troops broke and fled toward the Rio Grande.

Casualties:

General Arista reported 160 men killed, 228 wounded, and 159 missing. American reports of the battle put the Mexican losses as much higher, including hundreds who reportedly drowned while trying to cross the Rio Grande. They also lost seven or eight pieces of artillery, much ammunition, three flags, and about a hundred prisoners, including General La Vega. The Americans reported 33-45 men killed and 89-113 wounded, depending on the source.

Outcome:

The Battle of Resaca de la Palma drove the Mexican army out of Texas for the duration of the Mexican War.

Location:

Much of the Resaca de la Palma battle site is now covered by condominiums and businesses in modern day Brownsville. The battlefield is divided by the Paredes Line Road which crosses the Resaca in about the same spot the original bridge did. Areas to the east and west of the road preserve some of the positions of U.S. troops during the battle. Resaca de la Palma has been named a National Historic Landmark.

Markers:

A Texas historical marker describing the Battle of Resaca de la Palma stands on the north bank of the Resaca along the Paredes Line Road in Brownsville, Texas.

Texas Ranger/Comanche Battle
29 May 1850

Opponents:

Texas Rangers

> Captain John S. (Rip) Ford

>> Approximately 40 men

Comanche warriors

> Chief Otto Cuero

In May of 1850 Captain John S. Ford led a company of forty men on a scout between Laredo, San Antonio, and finally Corpus Christi. During their ride the Rangers fought a number of skirmishes with Comanches. At about 10 A.M. on May 29, the Rangers found the Comanches' trail. After following the trail for about five miles the Rangers discovered the Comanches' village and attacked it.

The Comanches abandoned the village when the Rangers charged, but fought back as they fled. Some warriors who had reached a high point could be seen by the Rangers as signaling to others of their tribe. The Rangers' attack faltered when William Gillespie was shot through a lung with an arrow. As Ford prepared to press the attack the other Rangers hesitated. They gathered around Gillespie because they feared the Comanches were trying to circle around to scalp him and steal his horse. The Comanches stood their ground while Gillespie was moved to safety. Meanwhile, the Rangers sniped at the Comanches trying to kill as many of their horses as possible.

When the Rangers' rear guard arrived they flanked the warriors' position and routed them. The Comanche chief, Otto Cuero, and another warrior gave their horses to wounded men to help them reach the cover of trees along Agua Dulce Creek. The "famous shot" or "shots" in this fight came when Ford wounded the retreating chief with a pistol shot at a distance reported to be 125 yards, and then David Steele finished him with a rifle shot from the same distance. The fight ended as the warriors reached Agua Dulce Creek.

Casualties:

The Comanches lost four men killed, including their chief, and seven wounded. The Rangers lost one man killed and two wounded.

Outcome:

This encounter was one of a series of events which eventually pushed the Comanches out of the Nueces Strip.

Location:

This fight took place in Jim Wells County not far from the present town of Alice.

Markers:

A Texas historical marker that states "Vicinity of Texas Rangers' Battle of May 29, 1850" is located on U.S. 281, 14.4 miles north of the town of Alice in Jim Wells County.

Hynes Bay
1852

Opponents:

Local Texan militia

> John Hynes
>> Approximately 30 men

Karankawa tribe
>> Approximately 50 men

The Karankawa tribe had returned to its old camping grounds along Hynes Bay after an absence of about eight years. When their camp was discovered by a settler a local militia company under John Hynes surrounded their camp and launched a surprise attack. In the ensuing battle the tribe met its final defeat on Texas land.

Casualties:

Most of the Karankawas were killed at Hynes Bay. The Texans spared a handful of men, women, and children.

Outcome:

The Battle of Hynes Bay drove the Karankawas out of Texas and into Mexico where they had gone before to seek refuge. It is believed that Hynes Bay was the last fight of the tribe on their home soil. Within ten years the Karankawas as a people were virtually extinct.

Location:

The battle took place in the vicinity of the former town of Hynesville six miles south of the present-day town of Tivoli in Refugio County.

Markers:

There is a Texas historical marker commemorating the "Karankawa Indians" at the intersection of Ocean Drive and South Alameda in Corpus Christi.

Rio Grande City (Cortina Battle)
27 December 1859

Opponents:

Texas Rangers and U.S. Army

    Captain John S. Ford (Texas Rangers)

    Major Samuel P. Heintzelman (U.S. Army)

        Approximately 370 men (122 regulars, 48 artillery-men, approximately 200 Rangers)

Mexican partisans

    Juan Nepumoceno Cortina

        350-400 men

On September 28, 1859, Juan N. Cortina, a border partisan leader and champion of Mexican rights, led a raid against Brownsville, Texas. Two months earlier, in July, Cortina had shot and wounded the city marshal of Brownsville while the marshal was arresting a man who had once worked for Cortina. Now, in September, Cortina sought vengeance on a number of individuals who he felt had been particularly hard on Mexicans and Mexican Americans along the border. By the time Mexican authorities convinced him to abandon the town two days later, three men had been killed and two wounded.

Texans retaliated by forming a militia group, "the Brownsville Tigers," and with the help of militia from Matamoras, Mexico, attacked Cortina's men on his family's ranch. The combined militia units were easily repulsed, and they only succeeded in losing their two cannon to Cortina's men.

Mexicans on both sides of the border rallied to Cortina while he continued to threaten Brownsville for the release of one of his men, who had been taken prisoner. When a company of Texas Rangers under Captain William G. Tobin arrived and hanged the prisoner, Cortina responded by ambushing and killing three of Tobin's Rangers.

These turbulent events set the stage for the Battle of Rio Grande City. The U.S. reacted to Cortina's growing power and menace by sending a force of regular army troops under Major Samuel P. Heintzelman and Texas Rangers under John S. (Rip) Ford.

Cortina's force retreated up the Rio Grande Valley with the arrival of the professional troops. The U.S. force pursued, with the Texas Rangers under Ford and Tobin catching up with it at Rio Grande City on December 27. Ford sent Tobin and his men to fight a holding action against Cortina's left while Ford attacked Cortina's right, along the Rio Grande. He also sent word to Heintzelman, who was trailing behind, to move his artillery forward and bring it into action against the center of Cortina's line. As the battle progressed, Ford's men sustained fire from three sides and were almost surrounded by Cortina's force. They managed to hold on and repulse a charge by Cortina's cavalry.

Cortina's men finally retreated from the field with the arrival of Heintzelman's regulars. Ford pursued the partisan force, and the battle ended with Ford's men capturing Cortina's two cannon.

Casualties:

The Texas Rangers suffered sixteen men wounded. Heintzelman estimated Cortina's casualties at about sixty men. Ford estimated them at about two hundred men.

Outcome:

Rio Grande City was a serious setback for Cortina. He retreated across the Rio Grande and set up a camp on a bend in the river called La Bolsa. On February 4, 1860, Ford crossed the Rio Grande and attacked Cortina at La Bolsa. Cortina fled deeper into Mexico where he remained for a year.

Location:

This fight took place at Rio Grande City in Starr County.

129

Markers:

There is a Texas historical marker on U.S. 83, Business Route Loop 254, in Rio Grande City, which identifies the "Site of Cortina Battle Dec. 27, 1859." There is another marker on U.S. 281 right-of-way, about twenty-five miles east of El Zacatal in Hidalgo County, which describes the "Battle of La Bolsa."

Chapter Five
The Civil War Years

THE CIVIL WAR

N

SABINE PASS

SAN ANTONIO

GALVESTON

NUECES

GULF OF MEXICO

CORPUS CHRISTI

RIO GRANDE

PALMITO RANCH

MATAMOROS

MEXICO

Nueces
10 August 1862

Opponents:

Confederate army (Second Texas Mounted Rifles; Texas Partisan Rangers; company of state troops; Taylor's battalion)

    Captain C.D. McRae

        94 men

Hill Country Unionists

    Major Fritz Tegener

        65 men

After Texas seceded from the Union, a number of Texas counties desired to remain loyal to the U.S. The citizens of these counties, many of them German immigrants to Texas, did not want to wage war against their home state, but neither did they want to be forced to fight for the Confederacy. The citizens formed a Union Loyal League and organized a battalion of three companies for their own protection. In July of 1862 Texas declared Gillespie, Kendall, Kerr, Edwards, and Kimble Counties of the Hill Country to be in active rebellion against the Confederacy. Rather than fight their fellow Texans, a group of Unionists decided to head for Mexico. They set out for the Rio Grande without any fear that they would be pursued.

On the evening of August 9, Tegener and his men camped on open land with a sparse cover of cedar trees about 150 yards west of the Nueces River. Only two guards were posted, and they were more involved in looking after the horses than guarding against an attack.

An hour or two before dawn a Confederate force under Captain C.D. McRae attacked the camp. The Unionists fought bravely and were able to repel two assaults. However, with an advantage in numbers and of firearms the Confederates eventually overran the camp.

Tegener was wounded early in the fight but managed to escape, as did a number of other Unionists. The Confederates acted with unusual brutality in this battle. One source states that one of two Unionists who stumbled upon the Confederates before the attack was questioned and then lynched. The handful of wounded prisoners taken were all executed. Another group of Unionists managed to escape as far as the Rio Grande. They were killed by Confederate troops while crossing the Rio Grande two months later.

Casualties:

The Unionists lost nineteen killed in the battle, nine executed after the battle, and six to eight killed while crossing the Rio Grande on October 18. Of those who escaped six were wounded. The Confederates lost two killed and eighteen wounded. McRae was one of the wounded.

Outcome:

The Confederate troops were obviously the victors in this needless fight. The only probable outcome of the Battle of the Nueces is that it convinced at least eleven of the surviving Unionists to later join the U.S. Army's First Regiment of Texan Cavalry Volunteers and actively work to defeat the Confederacy.

Location:

The site of the Battle of the Nueces is in Kinney County at a bend in the west fork of the Nueces River on Silver Lake Ranch. It is on private property and can only be visited by special arraignment with the owner. It is about twenty miles from Fort Clark and forty to fifty miles from the Rio Grande. It has been described as being accessible only after a difficult ten-mile journey though private ranch property.

For more information on the Battle of Nueces, one should visit the Old Guardhouse Museum at Fort Clark Springs in Brackettville, Texas.

Fort Clark Springs
   on U.S. 99
   PO Box 345
   210-563-2493
   Monday-Thursday 7 A.M.-7 P.M.
   Friday 7 A.M.-9 P.M.
   Saturday & Sunday 8 A.M.-6 P.M.

Markers:

After the Civil War the remains of the Unionists were collected and buried at Comfort, Texas. On August 10, 1866, a monument was dedicated to their memory. The monument's location is described as being near the high school campus. Comfort is located on the Guadalupe River about thirty miles northwest of San Antonio and about eighty miles northeast of where the battle took place.

Corpus Christi
13-15 August 1862

Opponents:

U.S. Navy
   Acting Lieutenant John W. Kittredge
      Approximately 100 men
Four companies of the Eighth Texas Infantry and local volunteers
   Major Alfred M. Hobby
      Approximately 700 men

Three days after the fight on the Nueces a battle took place at Corpus Christi which was as notable for its politeness as Nueces was for its brutality. Acting Lieutenant John W. Kittredge USN moved into Corpus Christi Bay on August 12, 1862, with a fleet of four vessels: the steamer

U.S.S. *Sachem*; yacht U.S.S. *Corypheus*; and the *Reindeer* and the *Belle Italia*, two captured Confederate sloops which had been converted into gunboats.

On the following day, under a flag of truce, Kittredge met with Confederate Major Alfred M. Hobby and announced his plans to inspect U.S. government buildings in the town. Hobby refused and Kittredge suggested that Hobby remove all women and children from Corpus Christi within 24 hours, after which time his fleet would land a landing force. Hobby requested 48 hours and Kittredge agreed as long as the time was used for evacuation and not military preparations.

After the allotted period of time, Hobby moved three artillery pieces, an eighteen-pounder and two twelve-pounders, into a battery which dated back to the Mexican War. The Confederates had no artillerymen among their number, so Felix A. von Blüher, a veteran of the Mexican War, and Billy Mann, a Confederate private home on sick leave, offered their expertise. Kittredge's only action during this time had been to move his vessels into battle formation.

On the morning of August 16 the Confederate batteries opened fire. The Union fleet returned fire until the *Sachem* and *Corypheus* sustained hits and then moved out of range for repairs. The two ships returned by midafternoon and continued shelling until nightfall.

Sunday the 17th remained quiet, but on Monday morning the *Belle Italia* moved to shore north of the Confederate artillery battery and landed a force of thirty men and a twelve-pound howitzer. Their plan was to take and silence the Confederate guns, and they advanced toward the battery under the cover of grape and canister shot from the ships.

The attack was met by Major Hobby and twenty-five men who turned back the Federal force. A cavalry charge, being mounted under Captain James A. Ware, was halted by Hobby due to the danger of the fire from the ships.

On the following morning the Federal ships sailed out of Corpus Christi Bay.

Casualties:

The U.S. Navy suffered one man wounded aboard the *Sachem*. The Confederates lost one man killed in the infantry charge against the landing force.

Outcome:

Corpus Christi was a victory for the Confederates and kept the Bay opened for their use. It was hailed throughout Texas as the "Vicksburg of Texas."

Location:

Corpus Christi is on the Texas Gulf Coast 150 miles southeast of San Antonio and 160 miles north of Brownsville.

Markers:

There is a marker at 401 N. Broadway in Corpus Christi which identifies the location of the Kinney Stockade. The artillery pieces used to defend Corpus Christi were moved to their battery from this stockade. There is also a Confederate Memorial in the downtown area. A Texas historical marker under the High Bridge at the end of Water Street in Corpus Christi describes the "Early History of The Port of Corpus Christi." It mentions the port as having been blockaded by Federal ships during the Civil War.

Galveston
1 January 1863

Opponents:

Confederate army (various units)

Major General John Bankhead Magruder

Colonel Thomas Green

Brigadier General William R. Scurry

U.S. Navy and Army

Commander William B. Renshaw USN

Colonel Isaac S. Burrell, Forty-second Massachusetts Infantry

Commander William B. Renshaw of the U.S. Navy took possession of Galveston Island in early October of 1862. After a token resistance in the form of artillery fire from Fort Point, the Confederate army abandoned Galveston as indefensible. A small detachment of U.S. Marines landed and raised an American flag on the U.S. Customs House in a symbolic gesture, then lowered the flag and returned to the fleet. The Federal Navy restricted itself to patrolling the harbor until Christmas Day, when it sent ashore three companies of the recently arrived Forty-second Massachusetts Infantry under Colonel Isaac S. Burrell. The inexperienced men of this newly organized regiment fortified a brick warehouse on Kuhn's Wharf at the end of 18th Street.

The Confederate army was not inactive during this time. Major General John B. Magruder had been made commander of the Texas district after having suffered difficulties in the campaigns in the east. He was determined to retake Galveston. The battle plan called for a combined land and sea assault The land force consisted of combined infantry, cavalry, and artillery units along with twenty cannon. The naval force was two steamers, the C.S.S. *Neptune* and C.S.S. *Bayou City,* converted into "cottonclad" gunboats; the C.S.S. *John F. Carr,* which acted as a troop transport; and the C.S.S. *Lucy Gwinn,* which carried wood for the rest of the makeshift fleet. The boats would also carry dismounted cavalrymen, "horse marines." The Fifth Texas Cavalry provided 150 men to the *Bayou City*, and the Seventh Texas Cavalry provided 100 men to the *Neptune* and 50 men to the *John F. Carr.* The land troops would initiate the battle and then the Confederate gunboats would move on the Union fleet.

On New Year's Eve night Brigadier General William R. Scurry led the Confederate land troops over the two-mile-long railroad bridge that connected Galveston Island to the mainland. The battle began when General Magruder himself fired the first cannon. This "famous shot" of Galveston came at 4:00 A.M. The Confederate troops moved in with one group assaulting the Forty-second Massachusetts' position at Kuhn's Wharf and the rest moving their artillery pieces into position on different streets of the city. The Federal ships immediately opened up a devastating fire of grape shot.

The Federal troops had prepared to defend Kuhn's Wharf by taking up some of the planking on the wharf, thus separating it from the shore line and leaving only one board as a path across. The Confederates were forced to wade out into the water with scaling ladders to assault the wharf. Their attack failed when their ladders proved to be too short and the fire from the Union ships too heavy.

The Confederate land attack faltered and had almost failed completely at dawn, but then their delayed gunboats finally arrived. The *Bayou City* attempted to ram the U.S.S. *Harriet Lane* but glanced off, causing damage to both vessels. The *Neptune* then tried but began to sink under the hammering of the Federal guns. The *Bayou City* swung back to the attack and this time succeeded in ramming the *Harriet Lane.* The two became locked together. The U.S.S. *Owasco* joined the fight and attempted to save the *Harriet Lane* but was turned back by Confederate fire.

The battle now began to quiet down, and the Confederates demanded the surrender of the Union vessels. A three-hour truce was agreed upon while the Federals decided what to do. During the truce the Forty-second Massachusetts, still besieged in the warehouse, asked the Confederates to be allowed to communicate with the Federal naval forces. This request was denied, which left them no other choice but to surrender.

Commander Renshaw used the truce to try to save the rest of his fleet. With white flags still flying, the Federal ships made a run for the mouth of the Bay. Most of the ships made it, but Renshaw's flagship, the U.S.S. *Westfield*, ran aground on Pelican Island. Renshaw, two officers, and ten crewmen were killed by a premature explosion while trying to destroy the ship lest it fall into Confederate hands.

The *John F. Carr*, although carrying no cannon, pursued the Federal ships but gave up after the ships crossed the sandbar at the mouth of Galveston Bay. The Confederates took possession of a few small supply vessels left behind by the Federals, thus ending the Battle of Galveston.

Casualties:

Confederate forces lost 26 or 27 men killed and 117-130 wounded. The Federal forces lost 5 killed and 12 wounded aboard the *Harriet Lane*, 13 killed, including Renshaw, on the *Westfield*, and 16 casualties aboard the *Owasco*. The men of the Forty-second Massachusetts at Kuhn's Wharf were taken prisoner, as were sailors from the *Harriet Lane*. The *Harriet Lane* was captured and the *Westfield* destroyed.

Outcome:

Galveston was a stunning victory for the Confederate forces. Even Sam Houston, who opposed Texas seceding from the Union, praised the victory. Galveston returned to the Confederacy and continued to be a haven for blockade runners. Also the Union was denied a base of operation from which campaigns could be launched into the interior of Texas.

Location:

Galveston Island is fifty miles southeast of Houston on the Gulf Coast. There are no exhibits or attractions dedicated to the Battle of Galveston, but the city boasts of a number of historical districts and vintage nineteenth-century buildings which can take visitors back to the time of the Civil War battle. The popular Strand National Historic District boasts one of the best collections of restored Victorian architecture in the U.S. One can search out locations in the city where significant events of the Battle of Galveston took place. Fishing boats can now be chartered at the foot of 18th Street where the Forty-second Massachusetts made their stand on Kuhn's Wharf. The Galveston Wharves now stand where Kuhn's Wharf stood. It is private property which cannot be visited. General Magruder made his headquarters at Broadway and 24th Street. Confederate units made their attack down Broadway. Lieutenant Sidney Sherman, son of one of the heroes of San Jacinto, was fatally wounded on 21st Street. The Confederate land troops on the Strand endured punishing fire from the Union fleet.

Markers:

There are two Texas historical markers in Sherman County on the northern border of the Texas Panhandle, far removed from Galveston, which state "County Named for Sydney Sherman, C.S.A." One is two-and-a-half miles south of Stratford on U.S. 287. The other is two-and-a-half miles northeast of Stratford on U.S. 54 at a roadside park. Both mention Sherman as having lost his eldest son in the recapture of Galveston, 1863.

State Trooper/Indian Fight
29 August 1863

Opponents:

Texas state troopers

    Lieutenant T.C. Wright

        12 men

Native Americans (possibly Comanches)

Lieutenant T.C. Wright and a small company of Confederate state troopers attempted to stop a larger group of Indian warriors who were driving a herd of stolen horses through Taylor County. The warriors had the advantage in numbers and a position on higher ground when the troopers attacked. They outfought the troopers, who were forced to give up the fight.

Casualties:

The troopers suffered two men wounded, including Lieutenant Wright.

Outcome:

The Indians got away with their stolen horses.

Location:

This fight took place one mile east of Buffalo Gap in Taylor County.

Markers:

There is a Texas historical marker describing the "Vicinity of Indian Fight" at Old Settlers Reunion Ground in Buffalo Gap, Taylor County.

Sabine Pass
8 September 1863

Opponents:

U.S. Navy and Army (four infantry brigades, six artillery batteries of the U.S. Army's Nineteenth Corps, one squadron of the Texas First Union Cavalry, four gunboats of the U.S. Navy, and twenty-seven transports)

General William Buel Franklin

General Godfrey Weitzel (commanding ground forces)

Acting Lieutenant Frederick Crocker (commanding naval forces)

4,000-5,000 land troops plus naval personnel

Company F, Texas Heavy Artillery (the Davis Guards)

Lieutenant Richard William Dowling

47 men

The Civil War battle of Sabine Pass is surely one of the more fantastic battles to be fought on Texas soil. It ranks with the Alamo as a "hopeless" last stand, and with San Jacinto as an unlikely victory against lopsided odds.

The battle came about as an attempt by Federal forces to gain a foothold in Texas and open the interior of the state to invasion. Sabine Pass, at the southeastern corner of Jefferson County on the Gulf of Mexico, was chosen as the point of attack. The Pass was defended by Fort Griffin, a triangular structure of timber, railroad irons, and earthworks. It had been built in March of 1863 by Confederate engineers and slaves. Two thirty-two-pounder cannon, two twenty-four-pounder smoothbore cannon, and two thirty-two-pounder howitzers made up the fort's rather unimpressive armament. Fort Griffin was defended by the Davis Guards, Company F of the Texas Heavy Artillery under Captain Frederick H. Odlum. The Guards' commander was twenty-five-year-old Richard "Dick" Dowling, a native of Ireland and a successful Houston businessman and saloon owner, more well known for his colorful drinks like the "Kiss me quick and go" than for his military experience. The Davis Guards were hand picked Irish cronies of his from the docks and saloons of Houston and Galveston. They had previously seen action in the Battle of Galveston on January 1, 1863.

The Federal plan for attacking Fort Griffin got off to a very shaky start. The plan, which was scheduled for the morning of September 7, 1863, called for the gunboat U.S.S. *Granite City* to anchor off the mouth of Sabine Pass and act as a signal ship for the rest of the armada. Once they had assembled, four of the transports carrying the infantry and cavalry were to land their troops, while the gunboats would keep the fort engaged in artillery fire. The plan began to go sour when Charles W. Lamson, acting master of *Granite City* mistook a Federal ship for the dreaded Confederate raider C.S.S. *Alabama*. Lamson panicked, left his post, and took refuge with his gunboat in the mouth of a river thirty-five miles east of Sabine Pass. This left much of the fleet cruising up and down the Gulf Coast as far as Galveston. September 7, the day scheduled for the attack, was wasted in assembling the dispersed fleet and formulating new plans. The new plan called for the gunboats to shell the fort into submission before landing the troops. In the early morning of September 8, the gunboat U.S.S. *Clifton* steamed across the shallow six foot deep water at the mouth of the Pass and lobbed twenty-six shells at the fort. Only two found their mark and did little damage. However, it convinced acting Lieutenant Crocker, commander of the naval force, of the fort's strength. This initiated yet another revision of the attack plans.

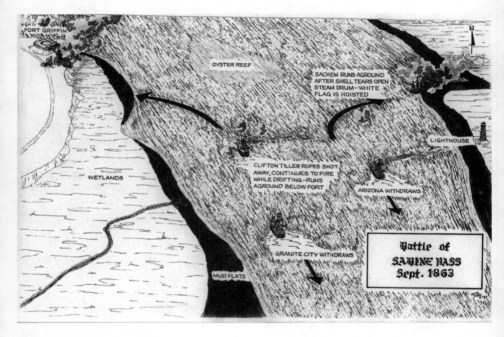

The revised plan now called for two of the Federal gunboats, U.S.S. *Sachem* and U.S.S. *Arizona,* to steam up the Louisiana (eastern) side of the channel to draw the fire of the fort, while the most heavily armed and armored *Clifton* followed by *Granite City* would steam up the Texas (western) channel and shell the fort. The troops would be put ashore south of the fort and attack over land.

The Davis Guards bided their time while the *Clifton* shelled their position. They wasted no shots by firing back. During the summer the Guards had driven colored stakes into the bottom of the Pass at 300-yard intervals. They sharpened their artillery skills by practice firing at the stakes and buoys. As a result the Guards had their guns accurately zeroed in on the two channels of the Pass.

The actual Federal attack did not get underway until 3:40 P.M. The *Sachem* led the way up the east channel and was immediately caught in a punishing fire from the fort. The "famous shot" of this battle came when Private Michael McKernan put a round from one of the twenty-four-pounder smoothbores right through the midships of the *Sachem*. Panic gripped the crew, and many abandoned ship to avoid the scalding steam from the gunboat's ruptured boiler. The *Arizona* had initially run aground on a mudbank but had managed to free itself. It followed the *Sachem* and lobbed a few shells at the fort. It then backed down the channel, ignoring calls for help from the *Sachem* when it was unable to pass the stricken gunboat. With the *Sachem* out of action and the *Arizona* retreating, Dowling's men were able to concentrate their accurate fire on the *Clifton,* which was steaming up the west channel. One shot tore away the gunboat's wheel rope, causing it to run aground just below the fort. The *Clifton* continued to exchange fire from the fort until its boiler was also blown up. The *Granite City* with Lamson in command never committed to the fight, and it approached no closer to the fort than the mouth of the Pass. In his haste to retreat, Lamson also convinced General Franklin that he had seen a sizable Confederate field artillery force approaching. The battle ended without the Federal landing force ever landing. In the rush to recross the sandbar at the mouth of the Pass and escape the imagined field artillery force, two transports ran aground. Over 200,000 rations and 200 hobbled mules were jettisoned in order to lighten their loads. What was left of the armada limped back to New Oreans.

Casualties:

The Union forces at Sabine Pass suffered 50-100 casualties, lost two gunboats with thirteen cannon, and lost 300-350 men as prisoners of war. The Davis Guards lost no men in the battle but several suffered badly burned hands from the guns, as well as slight powder burns and minor wounds from steel splinters. One of the fort's guns had been put out of service when it backed off its carriage.

Outcome:

The Battle of Sabine Pass was a resounding victory for the Confederacy, more accurately the Davis Guards. It prevented the Union from establishing an invasion point to the interior of Texas as well as preserving Sabine Pass as a valuable port for Confederate blockade runners. Dowling and his men became instant heroes in Texas. They were commended by Major General John B. Magruder, who authorized them to wear the word "Sabine" embroidered on their hats. They were congratulated by the Confederate Congress and by Confederate President Jefferson Davis, for whom the Guards had been named. A special silver medal was struck for the defenders, the only one of its kind issued by the Confederacy during the war.

Location:

The Sabine Pass Battleground/Sea Rim State Park is located fifteen and a half miles south of Port Arthur, Texas. It is a fifty-six-acre state park open during the daylight hours for picnicking, fishing, and boating. Not much of the site evokes the memory of the battle. The oyster bank which divided the channel has been dredged away. There are no original or reconstructed fortifications in place. As the Alamo now exists amid modern day hotels and malls, Sabine Pass is in the shadow of some intimidating oil and gas facilities. An open kiosk-type structure offers some information panels concerning the battle.

Sabine Pass Battleground Historical Park
   PO Box 1066
   Sabine Pass, TX 77655
   409-971-2451

Markers:

An impressive monument to the Davis Guards, topped by a statue of a barechested Dick Dowling, is located at the Sabine Pass State Park. There are also several Texas historical markers located together off a small parking area in the park. One of these commemorates "United States Forces at the Battle of Sabine Pass." Another remembers "United States Dead at the Battle of Sabine Pass." A historical marker dedicated to "Lieutenant Richard (Dick) Dowling" is located in Hermann Park in Houston. Another dedicated to "Sabine Pass-Richard Dowling" is located on State Highway 73, fifteen miles southeast of Port Arthur. A marker commemorating the "Site of Fort Griffin" is in Dick Dowling Park in the town of Sabine Pass.

Defenders of Sabine Pass as listed on the Dick Dowling statue at Sabine Pass:

Lieutenant Richard W. Dowling
Second Lieutenant N.H. Smith
Doctor Geo. H. Baily
Patrick Abbott   Pat Malone
Michael Carr   Alex McCabe

Abner R. Carter	Pat McDonnell
Pat Clair	Tim McDonough
James Corcoran	John McGrath
Thos. Daugherty	John McKeever
Hugh Deacan	Mich. McKernan
Michael Delaney	Dan McMurray
Dan Donovan	Jno. McNealis
Jno. Drummond	Mich. Monoghan
Michael Egan	Peter O'Hara
Pat Fitzgerald	Lawrence Plunkett
James Fleming	Maurice Powers
John Flood	Edward Pritchard
William Gleason	Charles Rheins
Tom Hagerty	Michael Sullivan
William Hardy	Pat Sullivan
John Hassett	Thomas Sullivan
John Hennessey	Mathew Walsh
James Higgins	John T. Westly
Tim Huggins	John W. White
Tim Hurley	Joseph Wilson
William L. Jett	

United States Servicemen killed at the Battle of Sabine Pass (Names of Federal soldiers and sailors interred after the battle as listed on the Texas historical markers at Sabine Pass.):

U.S.S. *Clifton*
    Actg Master-Executive Officer Robert Rhodes
    Signal Corps   William F. Pray
    Landsman   Michael Driscoll
                                A black "contraband"
    Missing and presumed dead:
    Twenty-one crewmen, mostly blacks, names un-
    known

U.S.S. *Sachem*
    Asst. Engineers   John Frasher
                                John Monroe

Crewmen

Henry Brown
George Houston
Peter Lee
William Robinson
Thomas Ryan
Randell Smith
Thomas J. Sullivan
Richard Turner
Calvin Williams
John Williams

Missing and presumed dead:
Crewmen

Isaac Carter
John Chace
Willis Green
John Horton
John Rolles
William Wilson

75th Regiment N.Y. Volunteers

Corporal
Privates

L.D. Hallock
H. Raymond
G. Beardsley
D.E. Parker
James M. Benedict
W.W. Miller

Missing and presumed dead:

Corporal
Privates

O.A. Brown
A.D. Borden
R.O. Canfield
F. Olford
R. Tucker
A.V. Brown
I. Bump

Ellison Springs Indian Fight
9 August 1864

Opponents:
Texan militia
>Lieutenant Singleton Gilbert
>>12-16 men

Native American warriors
>>Approximately 35 men

Lieutenant Singleton Gilbert led an attack of Texas militiamen against a larger party of Indians near Ellison Springs in Eastland County. The Indians were in the area on a raid for horses. The attack was repulsed by the warriors.

Casualties:

The Texan militia lost three men killed, including Gilbert, and three wounded. The Indian raiding party suffered no casualties in this fight.

Outcome:

This was an unfortunate waste of lives for the results. The Indians escaped with most of the horses. Later the Texans continued to follow them and recovered about eighteen of the fifty.

Location:

This fight took place near Ellison Springs in Eastland County several miles northwest of the town of Gorman.

Markers:

A Texas historical marker describing "Ellison Springs" and mentioning the fight is located on FM 8, three miles northeast of Gorman.

Elm Creek Raid and Fight
13 October 1864

Opponents:

Comanches and Kiowa raiders

Comanche Chief Little Buffalo

400-600 men in the raid, approximately 300 in the fight with the soldiers

Confederate army (Company D, Colonel James Bourland's Border Regiment) and civilians

Second Lieutenant N. Carson (in command of soldiers)

In the fall of 1864, Comanche and Kiowa raiders struck Young County, killing a number of settlers and carrying off captives. Confederate soldier Thornton K. Hamby, his father Thomas Hamby, and Thomas Wilson hid their families among some rocks on a cliff and then rode out to spread the alarm, with the Indians in hot pursuit. The three men made a stand at the ranch house of elderly George Bragg, protecting Bragg's family. Wilson was killed and Bragg and Thomas Hamby were wounded in the fight. The Indians discontinued the attack on the house at sunset.

While this fight was going on, another band of raiders drove a herd of stolen horses and cattle toward the Indian territory. They were pursued by Company D, under the command of Second Lieutenant N. Carson, of Colonel James Bourland's Border Regiment. Carson's men rode right into an ambush by about three hundred Indians and were forced into a retreat. During the retreat the Confederate troopers rescued two women at the McCoy house, bringing them to the safety of Fort Murry.

Perhaps one of the strangest scenes enacted in a Texas battle took place during the retreat. When the horse of civilian John Wooten was shot out from under him he took off on foot with two warriors riding after him. Every time Wooten stopped and leveled his gun at his pursuers, one of the warriors would call him by name and urge him to keep running. Wooten ran for three miles and escaped. He later assumed that the warriors were from the Comanche Reservation in Throckmorten County where Wooten had worked butchering beef for the reservation. Wooten felt that they had spared his life in return for his feeding them beef in the past.

Casualties:

The raiders lost approximately twenty men killed in the fights with the soldiers and at Bragg's ranch. Chief Little Buffalo was killed at Bragg's ranch. Carson lost five men killed and a number wounded. There were seven civilians killed in the raid. Bragg and Hamby were wounded. Two women and five children were taken captive.

Outcome:

The raiders made off with the seven captives and hundreds of horses and cattle. Later the captives were freed. Some accounts say they were freed through the efforts of Brit Johnson, a slave whose son was killed in the raid and whose wife and other children were taken captive. Johnson was said to have joined the Comanche tribe, gained the confidence of the tribe, and won the captives' freedom. Johnson was killed six years later, along with two companions, in a last stand against Kiowa warriors.

Location:

This raid and associated fights took place along Elm Creek in Young County in the vicinity of U.S. 380.

Markers:

There is a Texas historical marker off SH 24, nine miles west of Newcastle in Young County, which describes the "Indian Raid on Elm Creek, C.S.A." There is also a marker in Young County dedicated to Brit Johnson, and is located 1.3 miles west of his grave. It is located on FM 1769, 6.5 miles northwest of the town of Graham.

Adobe Walls #1
26 November 1864

Opponents:

First Cavalry New Mexico volunteers

Colonel Christopher (Kit) Carson

14 officers; 321 enlisted men; 75 Ute, Jicarilla Apache scouts; and civilian volunteers

Kiowa and Comanche warriors

Dohäsan (Kiowa), Stumbling Bear, Satanta (Comanche)

More than 3,000 men

The first Battle of Adobe Walls came about as a punitive expedition by New Mexico Volunteer Cavalry against the Kiowa and Comanche tribes of the Texas Panhandle region. The main reason for the expedition was to put a stop to raids by the tribes on wagon trains to and from Santa Fe. Another reason may have been to pit the Ute and Jicarilla Apache tribes against the Kiowa and Comanche tribes. The Civil War in the east had left a western military presence spread thin. There was a real fear that if an alliance was struck between the various tribes they would be unbeatable.

In early November 1864, Colonel Christopher (Kit) Carson's force, including twenty-seven wagons, plus an ambulance and two mountain howitzers, set out from New Mexico. The column's destination was the abandoned adobe fort of William Bent on the Canadian River. Carson was familiar with the site, having worked for Bent some twenty years before. The march was slowed down due to winter storms, and Carson's troop was not in striking distance of Adobe Walls until November 26.

Carson had pushed ahead with the cavalry and artillery, leaving the infantry and supply train following slowly. On the morning of the 26th he attacked the village of Chief Dohäsan, quickly putting the tribe to flight. The column immediately headed for Adobe Walls where his men positioned the howitzers and set up a hospital.

Word of the attack had already spread to the Comanche village by the fleeing Kiowas. One village was only about one mile away from the makeshift fort, and the combined strength of the Kiowas and Comanches proved to be much more than Carson had expected. Dohäsan led a number of assaults against the troopers' position with warriors estimated at over 3,000. Carson's howitzers, under the command of Lieutenant George H. Pettis, held off the warriors until late afternoon. By then Carson realized that his men could not hold their position indefinitely, and he withdrew in order to rejoin the infantry and supply train. The column was pursued by the warriors, but the howitzers again proved effective in holding them off.

Carson's group reunited that evening after he burned Dohäsan's village. On the morning of November 27, Carson broke off hostilities and led his column away.

Outcome:

Although Carson and his troop were forced to retreat from the field at Adobe Walls, they were not routed. The victory in this battle still must be assigned to him. Valuable buffalo robes and winter food supplies of the Comanches and Kiowas were destroyed. The Native Americans were also forced into the Medicine Lodge Treaty of 1867 in which they forfeited their rights to hunt north of the Arkansas River. The goal of pitting the Utes against the Comanches and Kiowas was also accomplished, thus preventing an alliance of the tribes.

Casualties:

Carson's casualties were reported as three dead and twenty-five wounded. Among these the Ute scouts suffered one dead and four wounded. The losses of the Comanches and Kiowas were originally reported as greater than sixty, with the number eventually being reported as high as one hundred to one hundred fifty.

Location:
The site of the first Battle of Adobe Walls is on private ranch lands in present-day Hutchinson County approximately eighteen miles northeast of Stinnett, Texas.

Markers:
A Texas historical marker describing this battle is located at SH 15 and FM 278, five miles north of Stinnett. It incorrectly lists the year of the battle as 1865 instead of 1864.

Dove Creek
8 January 1865

Opponents:
Confederate Frontier Battalion and Texas militia
Captain S.S. Totton
Captain Henry Fossett
161 men (Frontier Battalion), 325 men (militia)
Kickapoo tribe
400-600 men

In December of 1864 Texan scouts discovered an abandoned camp which they believed to be that of hostile Comanches and Kiowas. The camp actually was that of the peaceful Kickapoo tribe, who were migrating south to Mexico to escape the Civil War. The tribe was followed by a Texas militia force raised from Bosque, Comanche, Coryell, Erath, and Johnson Counties, under the command of Captain S.S. Totton.

Meanwhile, troops of the Confederate Frontier Battalion under Captain Henry Fossett gathered at Fort Chadborne and awaited the militia. After waiting two days Fossett left without the militia and set out after the Indians on his own. The two forces trailed the Indian camp separately but joined up on the morning of January 8,

1865, at a spot about one mile north of the Indians' camp on Dove Creek. Totton had about 220 men with him, having left the rest to guard and bring up the militia's pack train.

Fossett and Totton conferred and agreed upon a hastily devised battle plan. No one bothered to try to identify the Indian tribe or determine if they were hostile. Neither commander scouted the camp or prepared their men for battle.

The Indian camp was situated on the south side of Dove Creek. The attack on it began at about 9:00 A.M. on January 8. Totton and his militia circled to the east, waded across Dove Creek on foot, and struck at the center of the camp. Fossett and his mounted Confederates circled the camp to the west and captured the Indian horse herd. He also sent Lieutenant Brooks with about seventy-five men to attack the camp from the southwest in support of the militia.

The uncoordinated plan fell apart quickly. The Kickapoos had chosen a very good defensive position for their camp. They were protected by thick brush and heavy timber and two dry branches of the creek which made natural rifle pits.

When the militia attacked the camp they were met by withering fire by hundreds of Kickapoos wielding Enfield rifles. Three officers and sixteen enlisted men were killed in the opening minutes of the fight. The militia were driven from the camp in a full rout with about a hundred Kickapoos in pursuit. Brooks broke off his attack and rejoined Fossett. The Confederates took cover in timber but were separated into three groups. In midafternoon the Kickapoos almost succeeded in overrunning the Confederates' right wing but were repulsed.

An "infamous shot" was fired during this battle when an Indian came forward with two children and his hands raised. Some reports state that he was trying to establish that the Indian camp was friendly. Others say he was a prisoner. The Indian was shot and killed, possibly on Fossett's orders, or possibly due to a comment by Fossett that prisoners were not usually taken in Indian fighting, after which one of his men readily obliged.

The Confederates sustained fire from the Kickapoos until nightfall when they attempted a retreat. While they were crossing Dove Creek, they came under a heavy fire from the Kickapoos. They lost the Indian horse herd in the ensuing confusion, and their retreat turned into a rout.

The Confederates found the militia three miles away on Spring Creek. The two units camped there in the cold rain and heavy snow, butchering some of their own horses to stay alive.

Casualties:

The Confederate troops lost four killed and five wounded. The Texan militia lost eighteen killed and fourteen wounded for a total of twenty-two killed and nineteen wounded. The Kickapoos claimed to have lost twelve killed during the battle and two more who died of wounds when they reached Mexico. Fossett reported the Indian losses as twenty-three killed. Totton said their losses were more than a hundred.

Outcome:

This battle did nothing but incite the Kickapoos to vengeful raids against Texas after they crossed into Mexico. The raids continued for eight years. It was also a useless waste of life for both sides, especially for Texas at a time when the Confederacy was just about in its death throes.

Location:

The battle took place along the east bank of Dove Creek in Irion County, just west of the town of Knickerbocker in Tom Green County and about twenty miles southwest of San Angelo. The site is on private land and is not open to visits by the public. The best place for information on the battle is probably the West Texas Collection at Angelo State University at San Angelo. Also, the Tom Green County Main Library in San Angelo and the Irion

County Historical Society in Mertzon, Texas, are good sources of information on Dove Creek.

Markers:

A Texas historical marker describing the Dove Creek battle is located eight and a half miles southwest of Mertzon near the Irion County line.

Palmito Ranch
13 May 1865

Opponents:

U.S. Army (Sixty-second Colored Infantry, Thirty-fourth Indiana Infantry, Second Texas U.S. Cavalry)

Colonel Theodore H. Barrett

Lieutenant Colonel David Branson

Approximately 500 men

Confederate army (Giddings Texas Cavalry Battalion, Second Texas Cavalry, Benavides Texas Cavalry Regiment, six-gun battery of field artillery)

Colonel John S. Ford

Captain George Robeson (Giddings Battalion)

Approximately 490 men

News of Lee's surrender at Appomatox reached Confederate troops in the southeast tip of Texas on May 1, 1865, via the newspaper *New Orleans Times*, thrown from a steamer heading up the Rio Grande. Many of the Confederate troops left the army for home upon hearing this news. Others stayed on prepared to continue the fight.

At the same time Colonel Theodore H. Barrett, the Union commander at Brazos Island, received word that the Confederate forces were abandoning Brownsville. On May 11, 1865, he sent Lieutenant Colonel David Branson with a detachment of about three hundred men to occupy the town. Branson's men were spotted from the Mexico side of the Rio Grande by individuals variously identified as civilians, Confederates, or French or Mexican soldiers, and their presence was reported to the Confederate forces.

At Palmito Ranch the Federals were stopped by 190 Texas cavalrymen. After a skirmish both sides pulled back and made camp. At about 3:00 A.M. the following morning the Confederate cavalry reappeared and drove the Federals back to White's Ranch. Lieutenant Colonel Branson sent back to Brazos Island for reinforcements. Barrett arrived with 200 additional troops and briefly turned the tide. Once again they fought the Texas cavalrymen at Palmito Ranch and this time drove them back.

Later in the afternoon Confederate Colonel John S. Ford arrived on the battlefield with 300 reinforcements

Col. John S. Ford led Confederate troops in the last land battle of the Civil War at Palmito Ranch
(Courtesy of the Texas State Library and Archives Commission)

and six pieces of field artillery. At about 4:00 P.M. the Confederate guns opened up on the Federal lines with a coordinated cavalry charge against the right, left, and center of the line. The Federal infantry could not stand up against the Confederate cavalry and artillery on the open plains, and their battle line disintegrated. To cover their retreat the Federals left forty-six men of the Thirty-fourth Indiana Infantry back as skirmishers. They were swept up and captured by the Confederates. Next, 140 men of the Sixty-second Colored Infantry fanned out to cover the retreat and prevented the whole Federal force from being overrun. The Confederates pursued the Federals all the way back to Brazos Island. Ford only broke off the attack when more Federal troops came over from the island.

Casualties:

The Confederates suffered a few dozen wounded at Palmito Ranch. The Federal losses have been greatly exaggerated over the years. New evidence indicates that the Federals lost only one man killed but many more wounded. They also lost 115 men as prisoners, including four officers.

Outcome:

Palmito Ranch was a symbolic if not futile victory for the already defeated Confederacy. A few days later Confederate forces at Brownsville surrendered to Federal troops.

Location:

Palmito Ranch battlefield is located about fourteen miles east of Brownsville. Part of the land encompassing the battlefield is private land. Other portions are owned by the U.S. Fish and Wildlife Service.

Markers:

There is a Texas historical marker describing the Battle of Palmito Ranch on SH 4, twelve miles east of Brownsville, Texas.

Additional information on Civil War battles in Texas, including capsule histories of the battles, can be found at:

The Confederate Research Center
    Hill Junior College
    Box 619
    Hillsboro, TX 76645

Chapter Six

Native Americans' Last Stand

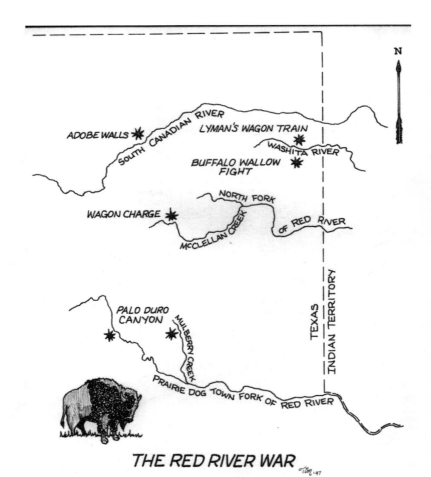

ADOBE WALLS

SOUTH CANADIAN RIVER

LYMAN'S WAGON TRAIN

WASHITA RIVER

BUFFALO WALLOW FIGHT

NORTH FORK

WAGON CHARGE

McCLELLAN CREEK

OF RED RIVER

TEXAS

INDIAN TERRITORY

PALO DURO CANYON

MULBERRY CREEK

PRAIRIE DOG TOWN FORK OF RED RIVER

N

THE RED RIVER WAR

Little Wichita River
12 July 1870

Opponents:

U.S. Sixth Cavalry

    Captain Curwen B. McClellan

       60 men

Kiowa warriors

    Kicking Bird

       Approximately 100 men

Kicking Bird led a party of Kiowa warriors off the reservation in 1870 on a raid against U.S. soldiers. His goal was to bolster his sagging prestige in the tribe. Kicking Bird had been trying to get along peacefully with the whites and as a result had been reviled as a coward by Kiowa warriors. Others who raided into Texas were thought of as heroes.

When word reached Fort Richardson in July that part of the raiding party had attacked a mail stage, Captain Curwen B. McClellan led out a force to stop them. He caught up with the Kiowas on July 11 and attacked their camp the next morning. McClellan had fifty-five troopers with him plus two officers, a surgeon, and a civilian scout. He soon found out that he was outnumbered by almost two to one, and also outgunned since the Kiowas were armed with Spencer rifles. McClellan's force was surrounded by the Kiowas with Kicking Bird leading attacks from all sides during the rest of the day. The soldiers only managed to escape that night after the warriors discontinued the fight themselves.

Casualties:

The Sixth Cavalry lost three men killed, one by a lance wielded by Kicking Bird himself, and eleven wounded. According to Captain McClellan the Kiowas lost fifteen killed. He could not give a definite count of the wounded.

Outcome:
Little Wichita River was a victory of pride for the Kiowa warriors. Kicking Bird restored his status as a warrior, and it was his last action in combat. He spent the rest of his life in peaceful pursuits.

Location:
This battle is believed to have taken place in north-western Archer County on the Little Wichita River. There is uncertainty about the exact site, but it is believed to be six miles northeast of Archer City and south of Lake Kickapoo.

Markers:
A Texas historical marker describing the "Battle of Little Wichita" is located at SH 25 and FM 210, two miles west of Archer City.

Texas Ranger/Indian Fight
1 January 1871

Opponents:
Texas Rangers and civilians
  Captain James M. Swisher
  Rancher Sam Gholson
    18 men
Native American raiders
    fewer than 12 men

Indian raiders, driving stolen horses from Coleman County, were attacked by a party of Texas Rangers and cowboys. After fighting all day the Indians finally left the horses and withdrew.

Casualties:

The Native Americans lost one man killed and several wounded. The Rangers and cowboys suffered one wounded.

Outcome:

The Rangers and cowboys retrieved the stolen horses.

Location:

This fight took place in the vicinity of the present-day town of Merkel in Taylor County.

Markers:

There is a Texas historical marker which states the "Vicinity of Indian Fight" on FM 1235, seven miles south of Merkel in Taylor County.

Blanco Canyon
9-15 October 1871

Opponents:

U.S. Army (eight companies of Fourth Cavalry, two companies of Eleventh Infantry, Tonkawa scouts)

Colonel Ranald S. Mackenzie

Approximately 600 men

Comanche warriors (Kotsoteka and Quahadi bands)

Quanah Parker

Colonel Ranald Mackenzie led an expedition against the Kotsoteka and Quahadi Comanche bands in the fall of 1871. On the night of October 9 Mackenzie and his men camped on the Fresh Fork of the Brazos near the mouth of Blanco Canyon. At about 1:00 A.M. on the following morning a Comanche war party charged through the camp driving off sixty-six of the cavalry's horses, including Mackenzie's. At sunrise a detachment of troopers followed

Col. Ranald S. Mackenzie
(Courtesy of the Texas State Library and Archives Commission)

a small group of Comanches, who led them into a trap. Lieutenant Robert Goldthwaite Carter and five troopers fought a holding action while the rest of the detachment retreated toward camp. By the time reinforcements arrived the Comanches had scattered.

Mackenzie and his men pursued the Comanches for the next six days, at times through a blinding snowstorm. When they returned to Blanco Canyon they skirmished with two Comanches, killing both of them. Mackenzie received an arrow wound to his thigh in this final action.

Casualties:

The U.S. Army lost one man killed and two wounded, including Mackenzie. The Comanches lost two killed.

Outcome:

There were no real victors in this battle, but Mackenzie and his men gained valuable experience in the tactics of the Southern Plains tribes which would aid them in battles to come.

Location:

This fight took place in Blanco Canyon near the White River in Crosby County.

Markers:

There is a Texas historical marker identifying the "Main Supply Camp on Historic Mackenzie Trail" located at a roadside park on U.S. 82, three miles east of Crosbyton in Crosby County. It mentions the Fourth Cavalry's 1871 campaign. There is also one identifying the "Mackenzie Trail" at the intersection of U.S. 60 and 385, 4.2 miles southeast of Hereford in Deaf Smith County. It briefly mentions Mackenzie's fight at Blanco Canyon.

North Fork of the Red River
29 September 1872

Opponents:

U.S. Army (five companies of the Fourth Cavalry, one company of the Twenty-fourth Infantry, Tonkawa scouts)

Colonel Ranald S. Mackenzie

231 men

Comanche tribe (Quahadi and Kotsoteka bands)

Kaiwotche

Approximately 262 lodges

During the summer of 1872 Colonel Ranald S. Mackenzie led a contingent of 300 men throughout northern Texas and into New Mexico in search of hostile Comanche bands. His goal was to stop the raids by Comanches in the Texas Panhandle region.

On September 29 he and part of his command (minus their supply train and guard) discovered a large Comanche village on the south side of the North Fork of the Red River. Mackenzie sent one cavalry company to capture the Indians' horse herd while the rest of his force charged the village in columns of four. The village was taken by complete surprise and was quickly routed. The strongest resistance came from a group of approximately eighty Comanches who made a stand near a water hole.

Casualties:

The U.S. Army lost two men killed and two wounded. The Comanches reportedly lost twenty-three killed, although there may have been more, and approximately one hundred thirty were taken prisoner. Of the prisoners, who were mostly women and children, eight died of wounds.

Outcome:

Mackenzie seized and destroyed a great deal of the Comanches' food, clothing, and supplies. His men also captured almost a thousand horses and mules, but most of these were recovered by Comanche warriors on the following night. More importantly, the battle shifted the balance of power in the Texas Panhandle away from the Comanche tribe and familiarized Mackenzie with the region for the battles still to come.

Location:

This battle took place on the south bank of the North Fork of the Red River, about seven miles from the mouth of McClellan Creek and east of present-day Lefors in Gray County.

Markers:

A Texas historical marker describing the "Battle of the North Fork of the Red River" is located on SH 273, ten miles southeast of Lefors in Gray County.

Deer Creek

August 1873

Opponents:

Civilian volunteers

    Captain Dan W. Roberts

        10 men

Native American raiders

    Approximately 33 men

The Battle of Deer Creek came about after Thomas Phelps and his wife were murdered by a party of Indian raiders on their ranch near Cypress Creek in Blanco County. The men of the nearby town of Round Mountain resolved to organize and battle the Indians if they returned. Within a few days a party of Indians were reported to the north and traveling toward Round Mountain. Captain Dan Roberts and a party of five men rode out to confront them. They were joined on the trail by Captain James Ingram and three others. The party was poorly armed, some only carrying revolvers.

When Roberts' men spotted a lone Indian disappearing over the top of a hill they charged around the hill in an attempt to overtake him. They rode right into an ambush set by the Indians who were hidden in a shallow ravine. Roberts' brother George was wounded in the first volley and was removed from the field. Dan Roberts attempted to flank the Indians' position in the ravine, but he also received a painful wound to his left thigh. He began to suffer so much from thirst that his men gave up the fight and carried him to a nearby farmhouse. Reinforcements under Captain Cicero R. (Rufe) Perry arrived, and the men returned to the scene of the fight only to find that the Indians had gone.

Casualties:

Dan and George Roberts were wounded in the Deer Creek fight. Perry's men reported finding four Indian graves along the trail as they followed the raiders.

Outcome:

Senator H.C. King was so impressed with Roberts' description of the fight that the Texas Legislature presented Roberts and his men engraved 1873 Winchester rifles in appreciation of their service to the state.

Location:

This fight took place along Deer Creek, approximately fifty miles west of Austin.

Packsaddle Mountain Fight

5 August 1873

Opponents:

Texan Civilians

James R. Moss

8 men

Native Americans (some sources say Apaches others Comanches)

17 men

James R. Moss, a Legion Valley rancher, organized a group of other ranchers to follow the trail of a party of Indians. The Indians had been raiding cattle and horses in Llano County. Moss and his companions followed the trail to the top of Packsaddle Mountain, where the Indians camped in relative security. Along with the men in the camp were two women and one boy.

The ranchers approached undetected, killed a guard, and then charged into the camp, separating the Indians from their horse herd. The Indians charged the ranchers

171

twice in an attempt to reach their horses but were beaten back both times. After their chief was killed, the Indians left the mountain top and disappeared.

Casualties:

The Indians lost three men killed. The ranchers suffered four men wounded.

Outcome:

The ranchers found 300-400 pounds of beef in the Indians' camp and recovered a number of stolen horses. This was the last battle between Native Americans and settlers in Llano County.

Location:

This fight took place at the top of Packsaddle Mountain which is about five miles south of the town of Kingsland in Llano County. Packsaddle Mountain is about sixty-five miles north of San Antonio.

Markers:

There is a Texas historical marker describing the fight on Packsaddle Mountain on SH 71, fourteen miles southeast of the town of Llano in Llano County. There is also a granite marker at the top of the mountain dedicated by the Moss family in 1938.

Adobe Walls #2
27 June 1874

Opponents:

Cheyenne, Comanche, and Kiowa warriors

   Quanah Parker

   Isa-tai

     Approximately 700 men

Civilian buffalo hunters and storekeepers

   No specific commander

     28 men and 1 woman

     On the morning of June 27, 1874, a combined force of the Cheyenne, Comanche, and Kiowa tribes led by Quanah Parker and Isa-tai attacked the trading post at Adobe Walls. This was not the exact site of the 1864 battle but

Quanah Parker of the Comanche Tribe
(Courtesy of the Texas State Library and Archives Commission)

was located about one mile north of William Bent's abandoned fort.

The tribes were responding to the relentless incursion into their lands by hunters who were decimating the life-sustaining buffalo herds. The Native Americans were also encouraged by the medicine man Isa-tai, who assured the warriors that he could render useless the bullets of the hunters and also belch forth a never ending supply of bullets from his stomach.

Their target was a sprawling complex of buildings, established in March of that year, that included several stores, a restaurant, a saloon, a blacksmith shop, and a corral. The defenders were made up of twenty-eight buffalo hunters and merchants plus the wife of William Olds, the manager of the restaurant.

The attack was not a complete surprise. For ten days reports of attacks on small parties of hunters had been filtering into the post. In the early morning hours of the day of the attack a ridge pole in James N. Hanrahan's saloon supposedly cracked with a loud report akin to a gunshot. The men pitched in to help repair the damage and were awake at the time of the attack.

Although the warriors failed to surprise the post, they were able to mount a lightning attack. Most of the people inside the post managed to get under cover in three widely dispersed buildings: Myers and Leonard's store was defended by a dozen men; Hanrahan's saloon, approximately three hundred feet to the south, by ten or eleven men; and Rath and Wright's store, two hundred feet further south, by six men and Mrs. Olds. Two brothers, the Scheidlers, were killed in their wagon in the first charge.

The marksmanship and heavy buffalo guns of the hunters blunted the attack of the warriors. Quanah and his men were only able to ride around the compound and fire at the buildings. The warriors finally broke off their attack but not before fatally wounding Billy Tyler. They kept up a siege for the next several days, making occasional sorties against the post.

On the third day, the twenty-three-year-old guide Billy Dixon made the "famous shot" of this battle. A group of chiefs were viewing the scene from a distant hill when Dixon managed to pick one of them off with his "Sharps 50." The distance was later measured at 1,538 yards.

The battle ended when Quanah, who had been wounded, withdrew with his warriors. As news of the battle spread, reinforcements began to arrive, and by the end of the week there were more than a hundred men at Adobe Walls.

Casualties:

The defenders of Adobe Walls lost four men, including William Olds, who accidently shot himself in the head while descending from a lookout post. A monument at the site lists six Comanches and seven Cheyennes who had been killed, but it has been estimated that as many as thirty to forty may have been killed.

Outcome:

The victory in this case must go to the defenders of Adobe Walls who were able to hold off Quanah's attack with relatively minor losses. The tribes succeeded, for a short time, in stopping the slaughter of the buffalo. The post at Adobe Walls was later abandoned, and by August of that year Indians had destroyed the buildings. The long-term effects of this battle were tragic for Native Americans. The fight ignited the Red River War of 1874-'75. The end result was the final decimation of the buffalo herds, subjugation of the great tribes of the Southern Plains, and their relocation to reservations in Oklahoma.

Location:

Adobe Walls #2 was fought about one mile north of the original Adobe Walls battle of 1864. The site is located on the Turkey Track Ranch 1.4 miles south of the ranch's headquarters and about 16.25 miles northeast of the town of Stinnett in Hutchinson County. The site is now owned by the Panhandle-Plains Historical Museum. This museum features artifacts and information on the Battle of Adobe Walls #2, as well as the following battles of the Red River War. The Hutchinson County Historical Museum in the town of Borger is also recommended. It displays a diorama of the Battle of Adobe Walls #2.

Panhandle-Plains Historical Museum
    West Texas A&M University
    PO Box 967
    Canyon, TX 79016
    806-656-2244
    806-656-2250 FAX
    Monday-Saturday 9 A.M.-5 P.M.
    Summer 9 A.M.-6 P.M.
    Sunday 1-6 P.M.
    Closed Thanksgiving, Christmas Eve, Christmas, New
        Year's Day
    Admission: Donation.

Hutchinson County Historical Museum
    618 N. Main St.
    Borger, TX 79007
    Monday-Friday 9 A.M.-5 P.M.
    Saturday 11 A.M.-4:30 P.M.
    Sunday 2-5 P.M.
    Closed major legal holidays.

Markers:

There is a Texas historical marker at the intersection of SH 15 and FM 278, five miles north of Stinnett in Hutchinson County, that describes the "First Battle of Adobe Walls." It also mentions the 1874 battle. There are two red granite markers at the site of Adobe Walls #2. One, erected in 1924, lists the names of the defenders of Adobe Walls. It is located on what was the north wall of the Rath and Company store. The other lists the names of thirteen Native Americans who were killed at the battle. It was erected in 1941 and is slightly south of the Rath store. There are also six Texas State Archeological Landmark markers at the site. There are three graves at Adobe

Walls. Jacob and Isaac Scheidler and Billy Tyler rest in a common grave just north of what was the Myers and Leonard hide yard. William Olds' grave is approximately 200 feet southeast of the Rath store. The grave of Billy Dixon is inside the south wall of the Rath store. His body was reinterred at the site in 1929.

Native Americans listed on the 1941 monument at Adobe Walls as having been killed in the battle:

Comanches	Cheyennes
Wild Horse	Chief Stone-Cay-Son
So-ta-do	Serpent Scales
Best-Son-In-Law	Spotted Feather
Wolf Tongue	Horse Chief
Slue Foot	Coyote
Cheyenne	Stone Teeth
	Slew Foot

Palo Duro Canyon #1
27-31 August 1874

Opponents:

U.S. Army (eight companies Sixth Cavalry, four companies Fifth Infantry, civilian and Delaware Indian scouts)

Colonel (Brevet Major General) Nelson A. Miles

Approximately 600 men

Cheyenne, Comanche, and Kiowa tribes

500-600 men

The attack on Adobe Walls opened up the Red River War between the U.S. Army and the Native American tribes of the Southern Plains. Five separate army commands converged on the Texas Panhandle. One of these was under the command of Colonel (Brevet Major General) Nelson A. Miles.

Major General Nelson Appleton Miles
(Courtesy U.S. Army Military History Institute)

As Miles's column entered Palo Duro Canyon from the south, his advance unit of thirty-nine scouts was attacked by about 75-200 Cheyennes. The scouts, which included Delaware Indians, were under the command of Lieutenant Frank D. Baldwin. The scouts dismounted and opened fire, forcing the Cheyennes to retreat to a bluff two miles away.

While the initial attack was taking place, Miles set up a battle formation with one battalion of the Sixth Cavalry on the right, another battalion plus the mounted scouts on the left, the artillery and one company of the Fifth Infantry in the center, and a company of the Fifth Infantry in reserve. As the force moved forward, Captain Adna R. Chaffee reassured his Sixth Cavalrymen: "If any man is killed I will make him a corporal!" For the next five hours Miles's men pushed the Indians back over twelve miles. The Cheyennes moved from one high point to the next, gathering Comanche and Kiowa warriors along the way until their number was between 500 and 600. Every time the warriors stopped to make a stand, Miles's men opened up on them with field guns and Gatling guns followed by a cavalry charge. The final charge by Captain Tullius C. Tupper's company of Sixth Cavalry pushed the warriors off a steep bluff and onto the Staked Plains. Miles broke off the fight since his provisions had run low and his force had fought after a gruelling march.

Casualties:

The Native Americans lost seventeen men killed in Palo Duro #1. The U.S. Army suffered two men, a sergeant and a Delaware scout, wounded.

Outcome:

Miles was able to destroy the Cheyenne village and much-needed supplies. Otherwise the battle was fairly indecisive.

Location:

This battle took place along the Red River in the Lower Palo Duro Canyon.

Markers:

There is a Texas historical marker describing the "First Battle of Palo Duro (Aug. 30, 1874)" in a roadside park on SH 207, twenty-six miles south of the town of Claude in Armstrong County.

Lyman's Wagon Train
9-14 September 1874

Opponents:

Kiowa warriors

> Lone Wolf
>
> Maman-ti
>
> Satanta
>
> Big Bow
>
> Big Tree
>
> Tohauson
>
>> Approximately 400 men

U.S. Army and civilian teamsters

> Captain Wyllys Lyman
>
>> 104 men

After the first Battle of Palo Duro Canyon in August 1874, Colonel Nelson A. Miles dispatched Captain Wyllys Lyman with thirty-six wagons and an escort to hurry along needed supplies from Camp Supply in the Indian Territory. While returning to Miles with the supplies, Lyman's force was attacked by a party of about seventy Kiowas. The fight lasted from afternoon until nightfall of September 9. Night brought a lull in the fighting, which allowed Lyman to fortify his circled wagons and get a messenger out to Camp Supply.

On the following day the Kiowas besieged the wagon train and kept the troopers from the only water hole. After two days the Kiowas began to lose interest and some drifted away. The arrival of cavalry reinforcements on September 15 hastened their departure.

Casualties:

The Kiowas' losses were estimated at thirteen men killed. Lyman lost two men killed and three wounded.

Outcome:

Lyman's men managed to hang on and survive this fight. There were no long-term results other than Lyman receiving a promotion and thirteen of his men receiving the Medal of Honor.

Location:

This fight took place in southeastern Hemphill County.

Markers:

There is a Texas historical marker on SH 33, twenty-one miles southeast of the town of Canadian in Hemphill County. It describes the "Site of Lyman's Wagon Train battle." There is a granite memorial at the actual site of the battle, which is about three miles southeast of the historical marker.

Buffalo Wallow Fight
12 September 1874

Opponents:

Comanche and Kiowa warriors

      Approximately 125 men

U.S. soldiers and civilian scouts

    Billy Dixon

    Amos Chapman

    6 men

Colonel Miles became concerned with the delay of Captain Lyman's wagon train and sent scouts Billy Dixon and Amos Chapman with four cavalry troopers to determine its whereabouts. This small party ran into Kiowa and Comanche warriors returning from the wagon train fight and were quickly surrounded. When the warriors shot one trooper and ran off the scouting party's horses, the scouts and troopers found themselves out in the open. After Chapman was hit in the knee with a bullet and disabled, Dixon led the other troopers to a nearby buffalo wallow which afforded some cover. They were forced to leave Chapman and George Smith, the trooper who had been shot, in the open. They protected the wounded men with rifle fire from the wallow. Later, Dixon ventured out and dragged Chapman into the cover of the wallow.

The warriors ceased their attack in the late afternoon during a thunderstorm. Peter Rath and Dixon then went out and dragged Smith into the wallow. They were surprised to see that he was still alive. He died a short time later.

The Kiowas and Comanches disappeared during the night, and a relief column of the Eighth Cavalry arrived the following morning. They only rendered the very minimum of aid and left the scouting party in the wallow to await evacuation. The party was finally rescued at about midnight on September 13.

Casualties:

The scouting party lost one man killed and suffered four wounded. Amos Chapman lost his left leg above the knee due to his wound. Chapman stated that no Indians were killed in this fight.

Outcome:

All six men were awarded the Medal of Honor for the Buffalo Wallow fight. Dixon's and Chapman's were later revoked since they were civilians. Dixon refused to give his up.

Location:

This fight took place between Gagely Creek and the Washita River in Hemphill County about twenty-two miles southeast of the town of Canadian.

Markers:

A granite marker was erected on the site in 1925 with the names of the six members of the scouting party. Billy

Dixon's Medal of Honor is on display in the Panhandle-Plains Historical Museum in Canyon, Texas. Many of Dixon's possessions are on display in the Panhandle-Plains Historical Museum and the Hutchinson County Historical Museum. For the addresses of these museums see Adobe Walls #2.

Palo Duro Canyon #2
28 September 1874

Opponents:

U.S. Army (two battalions Fourth Cavalry, Tonkawa scouts)

    Colonel Ranald S. Mackenzie

Native Americans (Comanche, Cheyenne, Kiowa tribes)

    Red War Bonnet (Comanche)

    Iron Shirt (Cheyenne)

    Poor Buffalo (Comanche)

    Lone Wolf (Kiowa)

Colonel Mackenzie and two battalions of his Fourth Cavalry located the camps of several tribes of Southern Plains Indians in Palo Duro Canyon in the Texas Panhandle. Mackenzie sent his scouts down the steep side of the canyon at about dawn on September 28 to spearhead the attack. They were followed by the Second Battalion. The First Battalion remained in reserve at the top of the canyon. The first camp was taken by complete surprise, but it and the others along the dark canyon floor were quickly abandoned by their occupants. The attack was so sudden that the troopers were able to seize almost all of the Indians' huge pony herd. Once the battle commenced the First Battalion joined the others on the canyon floor. The Indian warriors opened up heavy fire on the troopers from the canyon walls. Mackenzie's tight control of his men held them together, and they were able to push the warriors back. Skirmishing and sniping continued into the afternoon hours until Mackenzie ordered a detail to drive the warriors out of the cover they had taken. The battle ended with the destruction of the Indian camps. By 3:00 P.M. the cavalry was already moving out of the canyon.

Casualties:

The Indian tribes lost three men killed. The cavalry lost only one man.

Outcome:

Mackenzie's men seized 1,400-2,000 horses and mules from the tribes. Some were divided up by the Tonkawa scouts but the majority of them were shot. The Native Americans' camps were destroyed along with their supply of food for the winter. This battle marked the beginning of the end for the Southern Plains tribes.

Location:

Palo Duro Canyon extends some sixty miles across Randall, Armstrong, and Briscoe Counties in the Texas Panhandle. The head of the canyon is about fifteen miles southeast of Amarillo. The Indian camps were on the headwaters of the Prairie Dog Town Fork of the Red River in the vicinity of Canyon Chita Blanca.

Markers:

There is a Texas historical marker on SH 217 in Palo Duro Canyon State Park, twelve miles east of the town of Canyon, Texas. It describes "The Battle of Palo Duro Canyon September 28, 1874." There is also a marker on SH 86, seventeen miles east of the town of Tulia in Swisher County, which describes the shooting of the horses after the battle.

McClellan Creek
6 November 1874

Opponents:

Cheyenne warriors

Grey Beard

Approximately 100 men

U.S. Army (H Company Eighth Cavalry)

Lieutenant H.J. Farnsworth

25-28 men

Lieutenant H.J. Farnsworth led a patrol out of the camp of Major William R. Price on the Washita River, moving south toward McClellan Creek in early November 1874. On November 6, at McClellan Creek, his patrol was attacked by about one hundred Cheyenne warriors under Grey Beard. The troopers were pinned down, and the fight lasted from 1:30 P.M. until nightfall. Farnsworth's men escaped under the cover of darkness and were pressed so hard by the Cheyennes that they were forced to leave their dead on the field to be mutilated by their foe.

Casualties:

Grey Beard lost four to seven men killed and approximately ten wounded. The cavalrymen lost two men killed and four wounded.

Outcome:

The Cheyenne managed to take some degree of revenge against the U.S. Cavalry, but otherwise, the fight was indecisive for either side.

Location:

This fight took place on McClellan Creek just south of the present town of Pampa in Gray County.

Wagon Charge on McClellan Creek

8 November 1874

Opponents:

U.S. Army (one company Fifth Infantry, one company Sixth Cavalry, and civilian scouts)

Lieutenant Frank D. Baldwin

Cheyenne tribe

Chief Grey Beard

Approximately 200 warriors

On November 4, 1874, Colonel Miles sent Lieutenant Frank D. Baldwin with a train of twenty-three wagons to Camp Supply for much-needed provisions for his troops. Four days later, while the detachment was breaking camp on McClellan Creek, scouts brought in word that they had discovered a large Cheyenne camp of 100-110 lodges. Miles had given Baldwin the option of attacking or pursuing any hostile Indians he encountered on his mission.

On the morning of November 8, Baldwin arranged his wagons in a double column and filled them with infantry men. The cavalry and mounted scouts flanked the wagons. At about 8:30 A.M. Baldwin's bugler sounded the charge, and the column attacked the village in this unusual formation.

The village was taken by surprise The warriors managed to hold back the troopers long enough for the women and children to escape and then they fled after them. Baldwin and his men pursued them for four hours and over twelve miles. The Cheyennes rallied twice and made stands, but the soldiers always forced them to retreat. Baldwin halted the attack after the Cheyennes finally scattered.

Casualties:

Baldwin estimated that twenty Cheyenne were killed and an undetermined number wounded. Baldwin's men suffered no casualties in this engagement.

Outcome:

The U.S. troops rescued two children, Adelaide and Julia German, ages five and seven, respectively, who were kidnapped by the Cheyennes in Kansas. The children's parents, two brothers, and one sister had been killed, and their two older sisters had also been kidnapped. The older sisters had been in Grey Beard's camp but were taken out during the attack. They were later reunited with their younger sisters after the tribes had given up in the Red River War.

Location:

This battle was fought on the north branch of McClellan Creek near the present town of Pampa in Gray County.

Markers:

There is a Texas historical marker on SH 70, seventeen miles south of Pampa, which describes an "Indian Battlefield" and mentions Baldwin's rescue of the two sisters.

Yellow House Canyon
18 March 1877

Opponents:

Civilian buffalo hunters

"Lieutenant" Jim Smith

46 men

Comanche warriors

Chief Black Horse

Approximately 170 men

Quahadi Comanches under Black Horse had obtained a permit to leave their reservation and hunt in Texas in December of 1876. Black Horse used the opportunity to hunt buffalo hunters and take revenge on them for the destruction of the buffalo herds.

In March of 1877 a group of buffalo hunters in Rath City, fired up on whiskey and talk of revenge, formed themselves into a company under "Captain" Jim White and rode out to find the Comanches. White turned back after he became ill, and the command fell to "Lieutenant" Jim Smith. Only about half of the hunters were mounted; the rest rode in wagons where the hunters carried an abundant supply of whiskey to fuel their expedition.

After two weeks the hunters found Black Horse's camp in "Hidden Canyon." The mounted hunters divided and moved along the plains on either side of the canyon, while the dismounted men advanced down the center of the canyon.

The Comanches were caught by surprise when Smith ordered the attack but quickly rallied. Even the Comanche women took part in the fight, aggressively charging the hunters with pistols while their men found defensive positions. The fight continued until midafternoon. The hunters were finally forced to retreat after the Comanches set a grass fire and began to close in on them under the cover of the smoke. The hunters made it back to their wagons and set their own fires to cover their retreat back to Rath City.

Casualties:

The hunters suffered one man killed and two wounded. The Comanches' casualties were unreported by the hunters. A U.S. Cavalry patrol, that later went out after the Comanches, reported that thirty-five warriors died as a result of the fight and that twenty-two were wounded. However, it is unlikely that the boozy, undisciplined hunters could have caused so many casualties to the Comanches, and that the Comanches could have concealed so many losses.

Outcome:

This was the last fight between Native Americans and whites on the high plains of Texas. It also taught certain buffalo hunters a lesson in humility, if not sobriety.

Location:

The site of this fight is in the Canyon Lake Project in Lubbock, Texas. Mackenzie State Park in Lubbock encompasses a part of Yellow House Canyon where the force of buffalo hunters entered the canyon.

Markers:

There is a Texas historical marker in Mackenzie State Park at Double Mountain Fork in Lubbock. There are five plaques in this park that identify certain sites pertaining to the battle.

Tinaja de las Palmas
30 July 1880

Opponents:

U.S. Army (Tenth Cavalry)

Colonel Benjamin H. Grierson

Apache warriors (Warms Springs, Chiricahua, Mescalero bands)

Victorio

During the late 1870s and early 1880s Apache raids were on the increase in West Texas, New Mexico, and Mexico. Victorio and his Warms Springs Apaches had been assigned to a new reservation in Ojo Caliente, New Mexico, during this time. In 1877 the government suddenly moved him and his people to the San Carlos Reservation in Arizona, consolidating his people with their old antagonists, the San Carlos Apaches. Victorio would not stand for this move. He broke out of the reservation with his people and raided for two years. After he was captured in 1879, Victorio unsuccessfully attempted to gain permission for his people to live on the Mescalero Apache Reservation in New Mexico. The government had plans to send Victorio's people back to Arizona and to arrest him for murder and theft. Rather than submit to either, Victorio led a combined group of Warm Springs, Chiricahua, and Mescalero Apaches off the reservation and began raiding again. Colonel Benjamin H. Grierson led the U.S. Tenth Cavalry out to stop them in the spring of 1880.

Col. Benjamin H. Grierson
(Courtesy of Massachusetts Commandery Military Order of the Loyal Legion and the U.S. Army Military Institute)

Rather than chase the Apaches all over West Texas, Grierson assigned troops to various water holes that the Apaches relied on to wait for them. Grierson commanded the dispersed units from Eagle Springs, about one hundred miles from Fort Davis. When the telegraph between Eagle Springs and Fort Quitman, an abandoned post on the Rio Grande, went dead in early July, Grierson and a small detachment proceeded to Fort Quitman to investigate. This move also allowed him to take personal command of the campaign. While at Quitman, Grierson learned from Mexican troops across the Rio Grande that Victorio was headed north, back into Texas. Grierson decided to return to Eagle Springs to better coordinate his troops' movements. He set out on the afternoon of July 29 accompanied by his nineteen-year-old son, Robert, First Lieutenant William H. Beck, and six enlisted men.

The party reached Tinaja de las Palmas at about 7:00 P.M. Tinaja de las Palmas was not a natural spring but a catch basin for water runoff from the surrounding mountains. As soon as they arrived, a lone Apache appeared on nearby Rocky Ridge. Grierson sent a sergeant and two cavalrymen to drive him off. Couriers then arrived from Eagle Springs and reported several parties of Apaches in the area. Grierson realized that Victorio would have to come to Tinaja de las Palmas for water, since all of the other regular water sources were too heavily guarded. He decided to fortify Rocky Ridge with his small party and sent for reinforcements. His men constructed two small oval-shaped forts out of rocks at the top of the ridge. From this point they would be able to wait for reinforcements while covering the water hole.

On the following morning only fifteen men under Second Lieutenant Leighton Finley arrived with the mistaken idea that they were to escort Grierson and his party back to Eagle Pass. Grierson sent two troopers back with orders for all the available cavalry to converge on Tinaja de las Palmas. He also had Finley's remaining men construct another larger rock fortification at the base of the ridge.

At 8:00 A.M. the first Apaches appeared about half a mile to the south. Grierson ordered Finley to take ten of his men and keep the Apaches south of a stage road that ran east and west below the ridge. As Finley's men approached the Apaches, they were ambushed by another party of Apaches hidden in the brush near the road. Finley's men quickly dismounted and exchanged fire with the two groups of Apaches. Grierson and his party on the ridge were too far away to offer any help. Finley and his men held off the warriors for a half hour until two companies of reinforcements arrived from Eagle Springs. Companies C and G immediately joined the fight, but in the dust and smoke of battle they mistook Finley's men for Apaches and began firing on them too. Finley, now caught in a cross fire from friend and foe alike, had his men mount up and race back to the safety of their rock redoubt near Grierson. Miraculously they all made it back to cover with only one man wounded.

Companies C and G pressed their attack and briefly scattered Victorio's men. At the same time another company of reinforcements, Company A, approached from Fort Quitman. Victorio made one last attack before the reinforcement could arrive. Once again he was stopped by Companies C and G. When Company A arrived they turned the tide. Victorio and his men broke off the fight and disappeared into Quitman Canyon.

There would still be sporadic raids and skirmishes in the days and weeks to come, but the Battle of Tinaja de las Palmas was over.

Casualties:

The cavalry suffered one man killed, Private Martin Davis, and two men wounded. Grierson reported that the Apaches lost seven men killed and a number wounded.

Outcome:

This battle forced Victorio into Mexico and kept him from recruiting reinforcements from the reservations in the U.S. It marked the beginning of the end for him.

Location:

This fight took place below Rocky Ridge in present-day Hudspeth County about fifteen miles southeast of the town of Sierra Blanca. The site is on private ranch property and inquiries, researchers, and visitors are not welcome.

The Fort Davis National Historic site in Fort Davis, Texas, has displays and artifacts related to the Victorio campaign, including a diorama of the Battle at Tinaja de las Palmas. Fort Davis was the home to the "Buffalo Soldiers," black cavalrymen, most of whom were former slaves. The Ninth and Tenth Cavalry regiments were made up of black enlisted men and white officers. The Fort Davis site is located at the north edge of the town of Fort Davis about half a mile from the intersection of TH 17 and 118.

Fort Davis National Historic Site
  TX Highway 17/118
  Fort Davis, TX 79734
  915-426-3225
  915 426-3122 FAX
  Daily 8 A.M.-5 P.M.
  Summer 8 A.M.-6 P.M.
  Closed Christmas
  Admission $2

Rattlesnake Springs
6 August 1880

Opponents:
U.S. Army (five companies Tenth Cavalry, part of Company H, Twenty-fourth Infantry)
  Colonel Benjamin H. Grierson
    Approximately 200 men
Apache warriors
  Victorio
    125-150 men
After the fight at Tinaja de las Palmas, Victorio slipped back into Mexico but returned to Texas within days. Colonel Grierson, with five companies of the Tenth Cavalry

and twenty-five infantrymen, pursued the Apaches north toward Rattlesnake Springs. The troopers completed a grueling sixty-five-mile ride in twenty-one hours, beating Victorio's men to the Springs.

On the afternoon of August 6, 1880, the Apaches arrived and found two companies of cavalry guarding the Springs. The troopers exchanged fire with the Apaches and held them at bay until the arrival of two more cavalry companies. The reinforcements pushed the Apaches back into the mountains. Later in the afternoon the supply train and its infantry guard arrived. Victorio's men attacked the train but were driven back. They finally retreated under fire from the infantry and cavalry escort. Victorio gave up the fight and brought his men back into Mexico.

Casualties:

Three U.S. soldiers were killed and one was reported missing. There are a variety of reports on the Apaches' losses, combining those of Tinaja de las Palmas with this battle.

Outcome:

Rattlesnake Springs broke Victorio's power in West Texas. On October 15 he was killed by Mexican forces in the Tres Castillos Mountains of Mexico.

Location:

This fight took place in the valley between the Sierra Diablo and Delaware Mountains about forty miles north of the present town of Van Horn in Van Horn County.

Markers:

There are two Texas historical markers somewhat related to the campaign against Victorio, but they are in San Angelo, Texas, far removed from the scene of Rattlesnake Springs. One of these, at the Fort Concho National Historic Site, describes "The Tenth Cavalry," which was originally a regiment of black soldiers and white officers. The other describes "Fort Concho" and is located in front of the Fort Concho Museum.

Fort Concho is a National Historic Landmark in downtown San Angelo. It is a forty-acre site and contains twenty-three original and restored buildings. Among its many exhibits are those relating to the Indian campaigns in West Texas. There are no specific exhibits of the Victorio campaign at Fort Concho, but the research facility contains a good deal of material on this campaign and the Red River War.

Fort Concho National Historic Landmark
    630 South Oaks
    San Angelo, TX 76903
    (915) 657-4441
    (915) 657-4444 (tours)
    (915) 657-4540 (fax)
    Tuesday-Saturday 10 A.M.-5 P.M.
    Sunday 1-5 P.M.
    Closed on Thanksgiving, Christmas, and New Years
    Admission $2.00; $1.50 for senior citizens and members of the military; $1.25 for children ages 6-18
    Research facility opened by appointment only.

Appendix A

Some Texas Counties and Their Battles

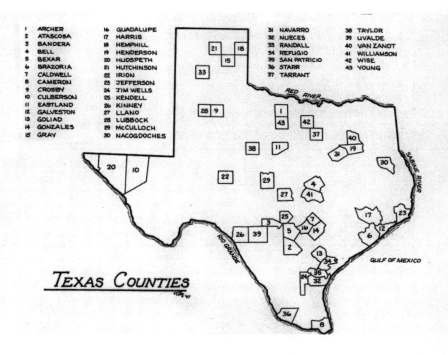

1	ARCHER	16	GUADALUPE	31	NAVARRO
2	ATASCOSA	17	HARRIS	32	NUECES
3	BANDERA	18	HEMPHILL	33	RANDALL
4	BELL	19	HENDERSON	34	REFUGIO
5	BEXAR	20	HUDSPETH	35	SAN PATRICIO
6	BRAZORIA	21	HUTCHINSON	36	STARR
7	CALDWELL	22	IRION	37	TARRANT
8	CAMERON	23	JEFFERSON	38	TAYLOR
9	CROSBY	24	JIM WELLS	39	UVALDE
10	CULBERSON	25	KENDELL	40	VAN ZANDT
11	EASTLAND	26	KINNEY	41	WILLIAMSON
12	GALVESTON	27	LLANO	42	WISE
13	GOLIAD	28	LUBBOCK	43	YOUNG
14	GONZALES	29	McCULLOCH		
15	GRAY	30	NACOGDOCHES		

TEXAS COUNTIES

RED RIVER

SABINE RIVER

RIO GRANDE

GULF OF MEXICO

County	Battle(s)
Archer	Little Wichita River
	Stone Houses
Atascosa	Medina
Bandera	Bandera Pass
Bell	Bird Creek Indian Fight
Bexar	Alamo
	Alazán
	Bexar
	Concepción
	Dawson Massacre
	Grass Fight
	Rosillo
	Salado
Brazoria	Jones Creek
	Velasco
Caldwell	Plum Creek
Cameron	Carricitos
	Palmito Ranch
	Palo Alto
	Resaca de la Palma
Crosby	Blanco Canyon
Culberson	Rattlesnake Springs
Eastland	Ellison Springs Indian Fight
Falls	Settlers/Indian Battle
Galveston	Galveston
Goliad	Coleto
	Perdido
Gonzales	Gonzales
Gray	McClellan Creek
	North Fork of the Red River
	Wagon Charge on McClellan Creek
Guadalupe	Córdova Rebellion Battle
Harris	San Jacinto
Hemphill	Buffalo Wallow Fight
	Lyman's Wagon Train
Henderson (and Van Zandt)	Neches

Hudspeth	Tinaja de las Palmas
Hutchinson	Adobe Walls #1
	Adobe Walls #2
Irion	Dove Creek
Jim Wells	Texas Ranger/Comanche Battle
Jefferson	Sabine Pass
Kendall	Walker's Creek (Pinta Trail Crossing)
Kinney	Nueces
Llano	Deer Creek
	Packsaddle Mountain Fight
Lubbock	Yellow House Canyon
McCulloch	Calf Creek
Nacogdoches	Nacogdoches
Navarro	Battle Creek (Surveyor's Fight)
Nueces	Corpus Christi
Randall	Palo Duro #1
	Palo Duro #2
Refugio	Hynes Bay
	Refugio
San Patricio	Agua Dulce Creek
	Lipantitlán #1
	Lipantitlán #2
	San Patricio
Starr	Rio Grande City
Tarrant	Village Creek
Taylor	State Trooper/Indian Fight
	Texas Ranger/Indian Fight
Uvalde	Cañon de Ugalde
Van Zandt (and Henderson)	Neches
Williamson	Brushy Creek
	San Gabriels
Wise	The Knobs
Young	Elm Creek

Appendix B

Some of the People Who Fought Battles in Texas and Some of Their Battles

Almonte, Juan Nepomuceno

(1803-1869)

Mexican army officer; member of the Mexican legation to London, 1824; member of the Mexican National Congress, 1830; editor of *El Atleta*; Colonel, Mexican army, Texas Campaign, 1836; General, Mexican army; member of the Mexican Legation to Belgium, 1839; member of the Mexican Department of War, 1840; Mexican Minister Plenipotentiary to Washington, 1841; Mexican Secretary of War, 1846; Minister Plenipotentiary to London, 1856; President of the Mexican Regency (under Maximilian); Mexican envoy to France (under Maximilian). Died in Paris on March 21, 1869.

Almonte's Texas battles:
The Alamo, 1836;
San Jacinto, 1836.

Arista, Mariano

(1802-1855)

Mexican army officer; member of the Supreme Tribunal of War; member of the Supreme Military Court; Commandant General of Tamaulipas; General of the Mexican Army of the North; Mexican Secretary of War, 1848; Constitutional President of Mexico, 1851. Died in Portugal on August 7, 1855.

Arista's Texas battles:
Palo Alto, 1846;
Resaca de la Palma, 1846.

Arredondo, José Joaqíun de

(1768-1837)

Spanish army officer; cadet in the Royal Spanish Guards, 1787; Colonel of Veracruz Infantry Regiment, 1810; Military Commandant of the Huasteca and Governor of Nuevo Santander, 1811; Commandant of the Eastern Division of the Provincias Internas, 1813. Died in Havana in 1837.

Arredondo's Texas battle:
Medina, 1813.

Baldwin, Francis Leonard Dwight

(1842-1923)

United States Army officer; winner of two Medals of Honor, one at Peachtree Creek, 1864 (Civil War), and one at Wagon Charge on McClellan Creek, 1874 (Red River War); Judge Advocate, Department of the Columbia, 1885; Inspector of Small Arms Practice, Department of the Missouri, 1891; Indian Agent, Anadarko Agency, 1894; Commander of U.S. 27th infantry, 1901; Commander of the Department of the Colorado, 1903; retired 1906; promoted to Major General, retired, 1915; Adjutant General of Colorado, World War I. Died on April 22, 1923.

Baldwin's Texas battles:
Palo Duro #1, 1874;
Wagon Charge on McClellan Creek, 1874.

Benavides, Santos

(1823-1891)

Merchant; rancher; political leader; soldier; Alcalde of Laredo; Procurador of Laredo, 1843; opposed Texas's annexation by the U.S.; Mayor of Laredo, 1856; Chief Justice of Webb County, 1859; served Confederacy during the

Civil War; Captain of the 33rd Texas Cavalry (the Benavides Regiment); Colonel of the Partisan Rangers; highest ranking Mexican in the Confederate army; served three terms in the Texas Legislature, 1879-1884; Texan delegate to the World Cotton Exposition, 1884. Died in Laredo on November 9, 1891.

Benavides's Texas battles:
Carrizo, 1861 (Second Cortina War);
Laredo, 1864.

Bowie, James

(1796-1836)

Texan soldier and adventurer; lumber man, ca. 1811 in Louisiana; served in the War of 1812 in a Louisiana Volunteer Regiment; slave trader; took part and was wounded in the "Sandbar fight" near Natchez, 1827; emigrated to Texas, 1830; member of an expedition to locate the Los Almagres silver mines, 1831; served in the Texas Revolution, 1835; Co-commander of the Alamo, 1836. Died in the Battle of the Alamo, March 6, 1836.

Bowie's Texas battles:
Calf Creek, 1831;
Nacogdoches, 1832;
Concepción, 1835;
Grass fight, 1835;
The Alamo, 1836.

Bowles (also known as Duwali)

(ca. 1756-1839)

Civil chief of several Cherokee villages in Texas, 1819; aided Mexico in ending the Fredonian Rebellion, 1827; negotiated a treaty with Sam Houston during the Texas Revolution, 1836 (this treaty was later invalidated by the Texas Senate). Killed in the battle of the Neches, July 16, 1839.

Bowles' Texas battle:
Neches, 1839.

Burleson, Edward

(1798-1851)

Served in the War of 1812; Colonel of Militia, Missouri, 1821; Colonel of Militia, Tennessee, 1823; member of the Ayuntamiento of Austin, Bexar, Goliad, and Guadalupe Counties, Texas, 1832; delegate to the Second Convention at Mina, 1833; member of the Texas Committee of Safety, 1835; General and Commander-in-Chief of the Texan Volunteer army, 1835; Colonel of Infantry, Texas Regular army, 1836; Colonel of Frontier Rangers, 1836; Representative to the Second Texas Congress, 1837-'38; Colonel, First Regular Infantry, 1838; Commander Frontier Regiment, 1839; Senator, First Texas Legislature of Texas, and President Pro Tem of the Senate, 1845; Major and senior aide-de-camp at battles of Monterrey and Buena Vista, Mexican-American War. Died in Austin on December 26, 1851.

Burleson's Texas battles:
Grass Fight, 1835;
Bexar, 1835;
San Jacinto, 1836;
Brushy Creek, 1839;
Córdova Rebellion battle, 1839;
Neches, 1839;
Pecan Bayou, 1839;
Plum Creek, 1840.

Carson, Christopher Houston (Kit)

(1809-1868)

Mountain man, trapper, explorer, 1829; hunter, Bent's Fort, 1841; hunter and guide for John C. Fremont, 1842; served in the Mexican-American War, 1846; Indian agent, Taos, New Mexico, 1854; Colonel, First New Mexico Volunteers, 1861; Brevet Brigadier General of Volunteers and Commander of Fort Garland, Colorado, 1866; Indian agent, Colorado Territory, 1867. Died at Fort Lyons, Colorado, May 23, 1868.

Carson's Texas battle:
Adobe Walls #1, 1864.

Cortina, Juan Nepomuceno

(1824-1894)

Rancher; served in the Mexican-American War (for Mexico); folk hero and champion of Mexican rights on the border; partisan leader; General of the Mexican Army of the North.

Cortina's Texas battles:
Palo Alto, 1846;
Resaca de la Palma, 1846;
Rio Grande City, 1859;
Carrizo, 1861.

Cos, Martin Perfecto de

(1800-1854)

Mexican army General; cadet, Mexican army, 1820; Brigadier General, 1833; veteran of the Texas Revolution, 1836; Commander at Tuxpan, Mexico, Mexican-American War, 1846; Commandant General and Political Chief of Tehuantepec Territory, Mexico. Died in Minatitlán, Vera Cruz, October 1, 1854.

Cos's Texas battles:
Bexar, 1835;
The Alamo, 1836;
San Jacinto, 1836.

Crockett, David

(1786-1836)

Veteran of the Creek Indian War, 1813; Justice of the Peace, Lawrence County, Tennessee, 1817; Town Commissioner, Lawrenceburg, Tennessee, 1818; Representative to the Tennessee Legislature, 1821; three-term Representative to the U.S. Congress from Tennessee, 1827, 1829, 1833; member of the Texas Volunteer Auxiliary Corps, Texas Revolution, 1836. Died in the Battle of the Alamo, San Antonio de Bexar, Texas, March 6, 1836.

Crockett's Texas battle:
The Alamo, 1836.

Dixon, William

(1850-1913)

Woodcutter, 1864; mule skinner, 1864; buffalo hunter, 1869; civilian army scout, 1874; awarded the Medal of Honor, Buffalo Wallow Fight, 1874 (later revoked); postmaster, Adobe Walls, Texas, 1883; sheriff, Hutchinson County, 1901; State Land Commissioner and Justice of the Peace, Hutchinson, Gray, and Roberts Counties; homesteader, Oklahoma, 1906. Died in Cimarron County, Oklahoma, March 9, 1913.

Dixon's Texas battles:
Adobe Walls #2, 1874;
Buffalo Wallow fight, 1874;
Wagon Charge on McClellan Creek, 1874.

Dowling, Richard William

(1838-1867)

Confederate army officer and businessman; saloon owner, 1857; liquor importer, 1860; 1st lieutenant, Company F, 3rd Texas Artillery Battalion, 1861; commanded the Davis Guards at the Battle of Sabine Pass, 1863; recruiting officer, 1864. Died in Houston on September 23, 1867.

Dowling's Texas battles:
Galveston, 1863;
Naval battle (aboard the C.S.S. *Josiaha A. Bell*), 1863;
Sabine Pass, 1863.

Fannin, James Walker, Jr.

(1804-1836)

Student, U.S. Military Academy at West Point,1819; plantation owner and slave trader, Velasco, Texas, 1834; Captain, Brazos Guards, 1835; Colonel, Regular Texan army, 1835; Commander-in-Chief, Texan army, February

12-March 12, 1836; Commander of Texan forces at Goliad, 1836. Killed in the Goliad Massacre, March 27, 1836.

Fannin's Texas battles:
Gonzales, 1835;
Concepción, 1835;
Coleto, 1836.

Flipper, Henry Ossian

(1856-1940)

U.S. Army officer; born into slavery, 1856; attended
Atlanta University; first black graduate of the U.S. Military Academy at West Point, 1877; assigned to the 10th
Cavalry, 1878; acting assistant Quartermaster, Post
Quartermaster and acting Commissary of Subsistence,
Fort Davis, 1880; dismissed from the army, 1882; assistant engineer for a surveying company, 1883; opened a
civil and mining engineering office, 1887; Special Agent
for the U.S. Court of Private Land Claims, 1893; editor of
the *Nogales Sunday Herald*, 1895; author; volunteered to
serve in the Spanish-American War, 1898, but the Senate
and the House of Representatives failed to restore him to
his previous rank; engineer and legal assistant to the Bal-
vanera Mining company, 1901; Assistant to the U.S. Secretary of the Interior, 1921; engineer for the Pantepec
Petroleum Company in Venezuela, 1923; retired, 1931.
Died May 3, 1940. Granted an Honorable Discharge from
the U.S. Army in 1976, dated 1882.

Flipper's Texas battle:
Tinaja de las Palmas, 1880.

Ford, John Salmon (Rip)

(1815-1897)

Texan soldier and ranger; served in the Texan army after the Texas Revolution, rising to the rank of 1st Lieutenant, 1836; practiced medicine, 1838; Representative of
the 9th Texas Congress, 1844; editor of the *Austin Texas
Democrat*, 1845; commanded a spy company during the
Mexican-American War, 1846; explored the territory be-

tween San Antonio and El Paso, 1849; Captain of a Texas Ranger company in the Nueces Strip, 1849; Member of the Texas Senate, 1852; editor of the *State Times*, 1852; officer of the Texas state troops, 1858; led troops in the campaign against Juan Cortina, 1859; Member of the Secession Convention, 1861; Colonel of the 2nd Texas Cavalry, 1861; led Confederate forces in the Battle of Palmito Ranch, 1865; editor of the Brownsville *Sentinel*, 1868; Delegate to the Democratic convention in Baltimore, 1872; Cattle and Hide Inspector, Cameron County, 1873; Mayor of Brownsville, 1874; Member of the Constitutional Convention of 1875; Member of the Texas Senate, 1876; Superintendent of the Deaf and Dumb School, 1879; author; historian; charter member of the Texas State Historical Association. Died in San Antonio, November 3, 1897.

Ford's Texas battles:
Texas Ranger/Comanche battle, 1850;
Rio Grande City, 1859;
Palmito Ranch, 1865.

Grant, Ulysses Simpson

(1822-1885)

President of the U.S. (two terms), U.S. Army General; graduate of the U.S. Military Academy at West Point, 1843; served in the Mexican-American War, 1846; assigned to Jefferson Barracks, Missouri, 1848; transferred to the Pacific Coast, 1852; resigned, 1854; farmer, real estate man, and store clerk; served in the Civil War, rising to the position of commander of all Union armies; 18th President of the U.S., 1868; retired from office, 1877. Died at Mount McGregor, N.Y., July 23, 1885.

Grant's Texas battle:
Palo Alto, 1846.

Grey Beard

(?-1875)

Medicine man, Southern Cheyenne; leader of the Dog Soldier warriors; fought U.S. troops in Kansas, 1857; consistently hostile to the U.S. until he turned himself in to the Brinton Darlington Agency in Indian Territory, 1871; led Cheyenne warriors in Red River War, 1874; surrendered, 1875. Killed during an attempted escape from a railroad car while being transported to imprisonment in Florida in 1875.

Grey Beard's Texas battles:
Adobe Walls #2, 1874;
McClellan Creek, 1874;
Wagon Train Charge on McClellan Creek, 1874.

Grierson, Benjamin Henry

(1826-1911)

U.S. Army Officer; music teacher and band leader, Jacksonville, Illinois, 1850; mercantile businessman, 1855; served in the Civil War rising to the rank of Major General of Volunteers; led a raid through Confederate territory in Mississippi, 1863; Commander, District of Northern Alabama; Colonel of the Regular Army, 1865; organized the 10th Cavalry, made up of black troopers; Commander of Fort Riley and Fort Gibson, 1867; Head of the District of Indian Territory, 1868; Commander of the District of the Pecos, 1878; led U.S. troops in the Victorio Campaign, 1880; Commander of Fort Davis, 1882; Commander of the Department of Texas 1883; Commander of the Whipple Barracks and Fort Grant in Arizona, 1885; Commander of the District of New Mexico, 1886; Commander of the Department of Arizona, 1888; promoted to Brigadier General and retired, 1890. Died at Omena, Michigan, August 31, 1911.

Grierson's Texas battles:
Tinaja de la Palmas, 1880;
Rattlesnake Springs, 1880.

Hays, John Coffee

(1817-1883)

Texas Ranger, surveyor; served in the Texas Revolution, 1836; Deputy Surveyor of the Bexar District; Colonel of a Texas Ranger unit in the Mexican-American War, 1846; Indian Agent for the Gila River Country, 1849; sheriff of San Francisco County, California, 1850; U.S. Surveyor General for California, 1853; helped found the city of Oakland, California; rancher; real estate man; delegate to the Democratic National Convention, 1876. Died on April 21, 1883.

Hays's Texas battles:
Plum Creek, 1840;
Bandera Pass, 1841;
Salado, 1842;
Walker's Creek, 1844.

Houston, Samuel

(1793-1863)

Political leader and president of the Republic of Texas; adopted member of the Cherokee tribe, 1809; served in the U.S. Army during the War of 1812, rising to the rank of First Lieutenant after the war; Sub-Indian agent, Cherokee tribe, 1817; lawyer, 1818; Adjutant General (Colonel) of the Tennessee Militia, 1818; Attorney General of the District of Nashville, 1818; Major General of the Tennessee Militia, 1821; Member of the U.S. House of Representatives from Tennessee, 1823 (two terms); Governor of Tennessee, 1827; resigned, 1829; lived among the Cherokees in Indian Territory; emigrated to Texas, 1832; delegate from Nacogdoches to the Convention of 1833; Commander of the troops of the Department of Nacogdoches, 1835; delegate from Nacogdoches to the Consulation of 1835; Major General of the Texas Revolutionary army, 1835; negotiated a treaty with the Cherokees during the Texas Revolution, 1836; delegate from Refugio to the convention, 1836; led Texan forces in the Battle of San

Jacinto, 1836; first elected president of the Republic of Texas, 1836; Member of the Texas House of Representatives from San Augustine, 1839; President of the Republic of Texas, 1841; U.S. Senator from Texas, 1846; Governor of Texas, 1859; removed from office for his opposition to Texas's secession from the Union during the Civil War. Died on July 26, 1863.

Houston's Texas battle:
San Jacinto, 1836.

Lone Wolf

(?-1879)

Kiowa chief; member of the Tsetanma Warrior Society and war leader, 1860; member of the Indian delegation to Washington D.C., 1863; signed the Little Arkansas Treaty, 1865; raided into Texas 1866; attended the Medicine Lodge Treaty meeting of 1867 but did not sign the treaty; war leader of the Kiowas, 1868; held hostage by Lieutenant Colonel George A. Custer and General Philip Sheridan to force Kiowas on the reservation, 1869; participated in the Warren Wagon Train Raid, 1871, and the attack on the government wagon train at Howard's Wells, 1872; delegate of a peace conference to Washington D.C., 1872; took part in the Red River War, 1874; surrendered, 1875. Died at Fort Sill in the summer of 1879.

Lone Wolf's Texas battles:
Warren Wagon Train Raid, 1871;
Wagon Train Attack, Howard's Wells, 1872;
Adobe Walls #2, 1874;
Lost Valley Fight, 1874;
Lyman's Wagon Train, 1874;
Palo Duro Canyon #2, 1874.

Mackenzie, Ranald Slidell

(1840-1889)

U.S. Army officer; graduate of the U.S. Military Academy at West Point, at the top of his class, 1862; served in the Civil War rising to the rank of Brevet Major General;

wounded six times during the war; Colonel of the 41st Colored Infantry, 1867; Commander of the 4th Cavalry, 1871; led one of the five columns of U.S. troops into the Texas Panhandle during the Red River War; Commander of the District of the Black Hills and Camp Robinson, Nebraska, 1876; led an expedition from Fort Clark into Mexico to put an end to border raiding, 1878; commanded six companies of cavalry in Colorado, 1879; commanded troops in Arizona against the Apaches, 1881; Commander of the District of New Mexico, 1881; promoted to Brigadier General, 1882; Commander of the Department of Texas, 1883; retired, 1884. Died on Staten Island, New York, on January 19, 1889.

Mackenzie's Texas battles:
Blanco Canyon, 1871;
North Fork of the Red River, 1872;
Tule Canyon, 1874;
Palo Duro Canyon #2, 1874.

Masterson, Bartholomew (William Barclay) (Bat)

(1853-1921)

United States Marshal; buffalo hide hunter, 1871; helped construct Adobe Walls trading post, 1874; took part in the Red River War as a civilian scout, 1874; teamster, 1874; buffalo hunter, 1875; badly wounded in shoot-out with Cpl. Melvin A. King, 1876; sheriff of Ford County, Kansas, 1878; Deputy U.S. Marshal, 1879; gambler and saloon worker, 1881; marshal of Creede, Colorado, 1892; Deputy U.S. Marshal for the Southern District of New York, 1903; author, 1905; sports editor for *The New York Morning Telegraph*. Died in New York on October 25, 1921.

Masterson's Texas battles:
Adobe Walls #2, 1874.

Miles, Nelson Appleton

(1839-1925)

General of the U.S. Army; store clerk, 1856; served in the Civil War, rising to the rank of Major General of Volunteers; wounded four times; awarded the Medal of Honor for gallantry at Chancellorsville; Commander of Fort Monroe, Virginia, 1865; Colonel of the Regular Army, 1866; Administrator of the Freedmen's Bureau in North Carolina, 1866; Colonel of the 5th Infantry, 1869; led one of the five columns of U.S. troops in the Red River War, 1874; campaigned against the Sioux, 1876, and Nez Percé, 1877; promoted to Brigadier General, 1880; Commander of the Department of Arizona, 1886; promoted to Major General, 1889; Commander of the Division of the Missouri; General in Chief of the U.S. Army, 1895; commanded the U.S. Army during the Spanish-American War, 1898; promoted to Lieutenant General, 1900; retired, 1903. Died on May 15, 1925.

Miles's Texas battle:
Palo Duro #1, 1874.

Quanah Parker

(ca. 1845-1911)

Chief of the Quahadi Comanches; war leader during the Red River War of 1874; cattle rancher; businessman; advocate of peace education and assimilation during the Comanches' reservation days; deputy sheriff, Lawton, Oklahoma, 1902. Died in Oklahoma in 1911.

Quanah's Texas battles:
Blanco Canyon, 1871;
Adobe Walls #2, 1874.

Santa Anna, Antonio Lopez de

(1794-1876)

Mexican General and five-time President of Mexico; cadet, Fijo de Vera Cruz Spanish Infantry regiment, 1810; served the Royalist forces against the Guitiérrez-Magee expedition, 1813; and the Mina expedition, 1817; shifted his allegiance to Mexican rebels, 1821; Military Governor of Yucatán, 1824; Governor of Vera Cruz, 1829; defeated the Spanish invasion at Tampico, 1829; President of Mexico, 1833; led Mexican forces into Texas during the Texas Revolution, 1836; taken prisoner at San Jacinto, 1836; returned to Texas via the U.S., 1837; wounded (lost leg) fighting the French at Vera Cruz, 1838; Acting President of Mexico, 1839; Dictator of Mexico, 1841; exiled to Cuba, 1845; President of Mexico, 1846; commanded Mexican forces in the Northern campaign, Mexican-American War, 1847; exiled, 1848; President and Dictator of Mexico, 1853; exiled, 1855; returned to Vera Cruz, arrested and exiled, 1867; returned to Mexico, 1874. Died June 21, 1876.

Santa Anna's Texas battles:
Medina, 1813;
The Alamo, 1836;
San Jacinto, 1836.

Seguin, Juan Nepomuceno

(1806-1890)

Texan rancher, military and political leader; Alderman of San Antonio de Bexar, 1828; Alcalde of San Antonio de Bexar, 1833; Political Chief, Department of Bexar, 1834; Commander of Cavalry Company, Texas Revolutionary army, 1835; Military Commander of San Antonio, 1837; Senator, Republic of Texas, 2nd, 3rd, and 4th Congress; Mayor of San Antonio, 1840; resigned as Mayor in 1842 and fled to Mexico due to the suspicion that he aided the 1842 Vásquez incursion into Texas; participated in General Woll's incursion into Texas, 1842; commanded a Mexican frontier defense unit during the Mexican-American War; returned to Texas after the war; Constable of Bexar County, 1850s; Judge of Wilson County, 1860s. Died in Nuevo Laredo, August 27, 1890.

Seguin's Texas battles:
Bexar, 1835;
The Alamo, 1836 (was present during the siege, but left as courier before the battle);
San Jacinto, 1836;
Salado, 1842 (on Mexican side).

Taylor, Zachary

(1784-1850)

U.S. Army General and President of the United States; Lieutenant, U.S. Army, 1808; took part in the defense of Fort Harrison, Indiana, 1812, the Black Hawk War, 1832, and the Seminole War, 1837-'40; Commander of the U.S. Army in Texas during the Mexican-American War, 1846; 12th President of the United States, 1848. Died on July 9, 1850.

Taylor's Texas battles:
Palo Alto, 1846;
Resaca de la Palma, 1846.

Travis, William Barret

(1809-1836)

School teacher; newspaperman; lawyer; cavalry officer, Texas Revolutionary army, 1835-'36; commander of the Alamo garrison, 1836.

Travis's Texas battles:
Grass fight, 1835;
The Alamo, 1836.

Ugartechea, Domingo de

(? - 1839)

Mexican army officer; cadet, Spanish Royalist army, 1813; Commander of Fort Velasco, 1832; Military Commandant of Coahuila and Texas, 1835; Commandant of Mexican reserves at Copano, Victoria, and Goliad, 1836. Killed at Saltillo, Mexico, May 24, 1839.

Ugartechea's Texas battles:
Medina, 1813;
Velasco, 1832;
Bexar, 1835.

Urrea, José Cosme de

(1797-1849)

Mexican army officer; cadet in the Presidial Company of San Rafael Buena Vista, 1809; Member of the Secretariat in command of Durango, 1829; Commander of the Permanent Regiment of Cuautla, 1834; Commandant General and Governor of Durango, 1835; Commander of Eastern Division during the Texas Revolution, 1836; Commandant General of Sinaloa and Sonora, 1837; Constitutional Governor of Sinaloa and Sonora; led Mexican troops in the Mexican-American War. Died in 1849.

Urrea's Texas battles:
San Patricio, 1836;
Agua Dulce Creek, 1836;
Coleto, 1836.

Victorio

(ca 1825-1880)

Leader of the Warm Springs Apaches; Apache war leader and border raider.

Victorio's Texas battles:
Tinaja de las Palmas, 1880;
Rattlesnake Springs, 1880.

Bibliography

Sources

The following abbreviations will be used in these sources:

SWHQ   *Southwestern Historical Quarterly*
TSHA   Texas State Historical Association
TSHAQ   *Texas State Historical Association Quarterly*

Archival Material:

[Ham, Caiaphas K.]. "Mr. Ham's Recollections of Col. Bowie." *Memoirs of John Salmon Ford*, I, 87-112. Ms. copy, Texas State Archives, Texas State Library, Austin.

Articles

Barr, Alwyn. "Sabine Pass, September 1863." *Texas Military History 2* (February 1962): 17-22.

Berlandier, John Louis. "An Eyewitness Account–Battle of the 8th Day of May of 1846, on the Plains of Palo Alto." *Palo Alto Dispatch* (15 April 1996): 1-3.

"Bowie's Official Report of San Saba Fight." *Frontier Times* 16 (July 1939): 425-427.

Canales, José T. "Juan N. Cortina Presents his Motion for a New Trial." An address delivered before the Lower Rio Grande Valley Historical Assoc., on October 25, 1951. *Juan N. Cortina: Two Interpretations.* Ed. Cortes, Carlos E. New York: Arno Press, 1947.

Cole, Melanie. "Goliad's Ghosts." *Texas Monthly*, April 1993, 48.

Connor, Seymour V. "The Battle of San Jacinto." *Battles of Texas.* Waco, Texas: Texian Press, 1967.

Crosby, David F. "Texas Rangers in the Battle of Brushy Creek." *Wild West*, August 1997, 60.

Davenport, Harbet. "The Men of Goliad." *SWHQ* 43 (July 1939): 1-41.

Day, James M. "Goliad." *Battles of Texas*. Waco, Texas: Texian Press, 1967.

Frantz, Joe B. "The Alamo." *Battles of Texas*. Waco, Texas: Texian Press, 1967.

Frazier, Donald S. "Sibley's Texans and the Battle of Galveston." *SWHQ* 99 (October 1995): 175-215.

Goldfinch, Charles W. "Juan N. Cortina 1824–1892: A Reappraisal." Master of Art diss., University of Chicago, 1949. *Juan N. Cortina: Two Interpretations*. Ed. Cortes, Carlos E. New York: Arno Press, 1947.

Haarmann, Albert W. "Mexican Army Shields of Honor, 1842." *Military Collector & Historian–Journal of the Company of Military Historians*. 48 (Spring 1996): 38-39.

Hatcher, Mattie Austin. Trans. "Joaquín de Arredondo's Report of the Battle of the Medina, August 18, 1813." *TSHAQ* 11 (January 1908): 220-236.

Henderson, Harry McCorry. "The Surveyors Fight." *SWHQ* 56 (July 1952): 25-35.

_____. "The Magee-Gutiérrez Expedition." *SWHQ* 55 (July 1951): 43-61.

Hodge, Larry. "Travel Texas History–The West Region." *Texas Highways*, September 1989, 42-57.

Kelley, Linda. "Battle of Bird's Creek." *The Story of Bell County, Texas*, 1988.

Lewis, Preston "Bluster's Last Stand–The Battle of Yellowhouse Canyon." *True West*, April 1992, 14-18, May 1992, 21-25.

Maguire, Jack. "The Marines to the Rescue." *Southwest Airlines Magazine*, January 1983, 34.

Mann, William L. "James O. Rice, Hero of the Battle on the San Gabriels." *SWHQ* 55 (July 1951): 30-42.

McChristian, Douglas C. "Grierson's Fight at Tinaja de las Palmas: An Episode in the Victorio Campaign." *Red River Valley Historical Review* 7 (Winter 1982): 45-58.

Nall, Arthur E. "Old Rangers Visit Scene of Conflict." *Frontier Times* 2 (September 1925): 33-34.

Nance, Joseph Milton. "Abel Morgan and His Account of the Battle of Goliad." *SWHQ* 100 (October 1996): 207-233.

Neighbours, Kenneth. "Elm Creek Raid in Young County, 1864." *West Texas Historical Association Year Book* 40 (October 1964): 83-89.

Peacock, Howard and Anne Garner. "Travel Texas History–The East Region." *Texas Highways*, September 1989, 2-5.

_____. "Texas in Rare Form." *Texas Highways*, September 1989, 7-21.

Pool, William C. "Battle of Dove Creek." *SWHQ* 53 (July 1949): 367-385.

Pfost, Richard A. "War with Mexico!–The Campaign in Northern Mexico." *Command–Military History, Strategy & Analysis* 40 (November 1996): 20-32.

Proctor, Ben. "Palo Alto." *Battles of Texas*. Waco, Texas: Texian Press, 1967.

Richardson, Rupert N. "The Battle of Adobe Walls, 1874." *Battles of Texas*. Waco, Texas: Texian Press, 1967.

Rippy, Fred J. "Border Troubles along the Rio Grande, 1848 - 1860." *SWHQ* 23 (October 1919): 91-111.

Rullman, Elizabeth. "Dick Dowling and His Forty-three Irishmen." *Frontier Times* 16 (July 1939): 421-424.

Sherley, Connie. "Travel Texas History–The Central Region." *Texas Highways*, September 1989, 22-36.

Shook, Robert W. "The Battle of the Nueces, August 10. 1862." *SWHQ* 66 (July 1962): 32-40.

Simpson, Col. Harold B. "The Battle of Sabine Pass." *Battles of Texas*. Waco, Texas: Texian Press, 1967.

Simpson, James R. "The Battle of Sabine Pass." *Frontier Times*, 21 (August 1944): 419-422.

Spellmann, L.U., Editor. "Letters of the 'Dawson Men' from Perote Prison Mexico, 1842-1843." *SWHQ* 38 (April 1935): 246-269.

Steinbach, Robert H. "The Red River War of 1874-1875; Selected Correspondence between Lieutenant Frank Baldwin and His Wife, Alice." *SWHQ* 93 (April 1990): 497-518.

"Texas Independence Trail–A Special Advertising Supplement." *Texas Monthly*, April 1991, 93-103.

Tilloson, Cyrus. "The Battle of Agua Dulce." *Frontier Times* 25 (December 1947): 86-89.

Thorpe, Helen. "Historical Friction." *Texas Monthly*, October 1997, 74.

Tudor, W.G. "Ghost Writers of the Palo Duro." *SWHQ* (April 1996): 532-541.

Walker, Henry P., ed. "William McLane's Narrative of the Magee-Gutiérrez Expedition, 1812–1813. *SWHQ* 66 (October 1962): 234-251; 67 (January 1963): 457-479, and (April 1963): 569-588.

Westmoreland, Jr., Peck. "The Battle of Plum Creek." *Battles of Texas*. Waco, Texas: Texian Press, 1967.

Winfrey, Dorman H. "The Battle of the Neches." *Battles of Texas*. Waco, Texas: Texian Press, 1967.

Young, Jo. "The Battle of Sabine Pass." *SWHQ* 52 (July 1948): 398-409.

Books

Awbrey, Betty Dooley, Claude Dooley, and The Texas Historical Commission. *Why Stop?*. Houston: Gulf Publishing Company, 1978. Reprint, 1992.

Baker, T. Lindsay and Billy R. Harrison. with a Foreword by B. Byron Price. *Adobe Walls-The History and Archeology of the 1874 Trading Post*. College Station, Texas: Texas A&M University Press, 1986.

Barr, Alwyn. *Texans in Revolt-The Battle for San Antonio,* 1835. Austin: University of Texas Press, 1990.✗

Blake, R.B. *Nacogdoches.* Nacogdoches, Texas: The Nacogdoches Historical Society, 1939.

Branda, Eldon Stephen, ed. Foreword by Joe B. Frantz. *Handbook of Texas-A Supplement.* Austin: The TSHA, 1976.

Cobb, Hubbard. *American Battlefields.* New York: Macmillan, 1995.✗

Eisenhower, John S.D. *So Far From God-The U.S. War with Mexico.* New York: Random House, 1989.

Fehrenbach, T.R. *Comanches-The Destruction of a People.* New York: Alfred A. Knopf, 1974.

_____. *Lone Star-A History of Texas and the Texans.* New York: Macmillan Publishing Co., Inc., 1968.

Ford, John Salmon. With an introduction by Stephen B. Oates. *Rip Ford's Texas.* Austin: University of Texas Press, 1987.

Foote, Shelby. *The Civil War-Fort Sumter to Perryville.* New York: Vintage, 1989.

_____. *The Civil War-Red River to Appomattox.* New York: Vintage, 1989.

Gallaway, B.P. *Texas the Dark Corner of the Confederacy.* Lincoln, Nebraska and London: University of Nebraska Press, 1994.

Green, Rena Maverick, ed. *Samuel Maverick, Texan: 1803-1870.* San Antonio: The Corona Publishing Co., 1952.

Gregg, Rosalie. ed. *Wise County History-A Link With the Past.* n.p.: Nortex Press, 1975.

Haley, James L. *Apaches: A History and Culture Portrait.* Garden City, New York: Doubleday & Co., Inc., 1981.

_____. *The Buffalo War.* Garden City, New York: Doubleday & Company, Inc., 1976.

Harris, Theodore D. ed. *Negro Frontiersman: The Western Memoirs of Henry O. Flipper.* El Paso: Texas Western College Press, 1963.

Herring, Patricia Roche. *General José Cosme Urrea-His Life and Times 1797-1849.* Spokane, Washington: The Arthur H. Clarke Company, 1995.

Houston, Major General Sam. *Documents of Major General Sam Houston, Commander in Chief of the Texian Army to His Excellency David G. Burnett, president of the Republic of Texas; containing a detailed account of the Battle of San Jacinto.* New Orleans: John Cox & Co., Printers, 1836; reprint, Austin: The Pemberton Press, 1964.

Jenkins, John H. ed. *Papers of the Texas Revolution 1835-1836.* 10 Vols. Austin: Presidial Press, 1973.

Josephy, Jr., Alvin M. *The Civil War in the American West.* New York: Alfred A. Knopf, 1991.

Nance, Joseph Milton. *Attack and Counter Attack-The Texas-Mexican Frontier,* 1842. Austin: University of Texas Press, 1964.

National Parks: Index 1995. Washington D.C.: Office of Public Affairs and the Division of Publications, National Park Service, 1995.

Nevin, David. *The Mexican War.* New York: Time-Life Books, 1978.

_____. *The Texans.* New York: Time-Life Books, 1975.

Nichols, Edward J. *Zach Taylor's Little Army.* Garden City, New York: Doubleday & Company, Inc., 1963.

Palo Alto Battlefield National Historic Site–General Management Plan Environmental Assessment. Washington D.C.: United States Department of the Interior, National Park Service, n.d.

Pierce, Michael D. *The Most Promising Young Officer: A Life of Ranald Slidell Mackenzie.* Norman, Oklahoma: University of Oklahoma Press, 1993.

Pohl, James W. *The Battle of San Jacinto.* Austin: TSHA, 1989.

Pool, William C., maps by Edward Triggs and Lance Wren. *Historical Atlas of Texas.* Austin: The Encino Press, 1975.

Public Involvement Booklet–Palo Alto Battlefield National Historic Site. Washington D.C.: U.S. Government Printing Office, 1993.

Roell, Craig H. *Remember Goliad!* Austin: TSHA, 1994.

Sanchez, Ph.D., R.A., Mario L. *A Shared Experience–The History, Architecture and Historic Designations of the Lower Rio Grande Heritage Corridor.* Austin: Los Laminos del Rio Heritage Project and the Texas Historical Commission, 1994.

Sansom, John W. *Battle of Nueces River-in Kinney County, Texas, August 10th 1862.* San Antonio: n.p., 1905.

Schwarz, Ted. Robert H. Thonhoff, ed. and annotator. *Forgotten Battlefield of the First Texas Revolution-The Battle of the Medina, August 18, 1813.* Austin: Eakin Press, 1985.

Sowell, A.J. *Rangers and Pioneers of Texas.* New York: Argosy–Antiquarian Ltd., 1964.

_____. *Texas Indian Fighters.* Austin: Ben C. Jones & Co., printers, 1900; reprint, Austin: State House Press, 1986.

Tolbert, Frank X. *Day of San Jacinto.* New York, Toronto, & London: McGraw-Hill Book Company, Inc., 1959.

_____. *Dick Dowling at Sabine Pass.* New York, Toronto & London: McGraw-Hill Book Company, Inc., 1962.

Tyler, George W. *History of Bell County.* Belton, Texas: Dayton Kelley, 1966.

Tyler, Ron, Douglas E. Barnett, Roy R. Barkley, Penelope C. Anderson, Mark F. Odintz. eds. *The New Handbook of Texas.* 6 Vols. Austin: The TSHA, 1996.

Utley, Robert M. *Frontier Regulars-The United States Army and the Indians, 1886 -1890.* New York: Macmillan Publishing Co., Inc., 1973.

Wallace, Ernest. *Ranald S. Mackenzie on the Texas Frontier*. Lubbock, Texas: West Texas Museum Assoc., 1964.

Warren, Harris Gaylord. *The Sword Was Their Passport*. n.p.: Louisiana State University Press, 1943; reprint, Port Washington, N.Y. & London: Kennikat Press, 1972.

Webb, Walter Prescott, H. Bailey Carroll, Llerena B. Friend, Mary Joe Carroll, Louise Nolen. eds. *Handbook of Texas*. 2 Vols. Austin: The TSHA, 1952.

Wertz, Jay & Edwin C. Bearss. *Smithsonian's Great Battles and Battlefields of the Civil War*. New York: William Morrow and Company, Inc., 1997.

White, Lonnie J., et al. *Hostiles and Horse Soldiers*. Boulder, Colorado: Pruett Publishing Co., 1972.

Wilbarger, J.W. *Indian Depredations in Texas*. Austin: Hutchings Printing House, 1889: reprint, State House Press, 1985.

Workers of the Writers' Program of the Work Projects Administration in the State of Texas. With a Preface by J. Frank Davis. *Texas–A Guide to the Lone Star State*. New York: Hastings House Publishers, 1940.

Wooster, Ralph A. *Texas and Texans in the Civil War*. Austin: Eakin Press, 1995.

Yoakum, Esq., Henderson K. *History of Texas from its First Settlement in 1685 to its Annexation to the United States in 1846*. Vol. I. New York: Redfield, 1850.

Brochures

Battle of Palo Alto. Palo Alto Battlefield. National Historic Site. National Park Service. U.S. Department of the Interior.

Brady the Geographic Center of Texas. n.p.: Brady & McCulloch Co. Chamber of Commerce, n.d.

Brazosport Chamber of Commerce. *The Battle of Velasco*. Brazosport, Texas: Brazosport Chamber of Commerce, n.d.

Carricitos. Palo Alto Battlefield. National Historic Site. National Park Service. U.S. Department of the Interior.

Daughters of the Republic of Texas. *The Story of the Alamo-Thirteen Fateful Days in 1836.* n.p.: Daughters of the Republic of Texas, 1997.

Dawson, Joseph P. *The U.S.-Mexican War.* Washington D.C.: National Parks and Conservation Association, 1996.

Fannin Battleground State Historical Park–Texas Revolution Site of the Battle of Coleto, March 19, 1836. n.p.: Texas Parks and Wildlife Department, n.d.

Fort Brown. Palo Alto Battlefield. National Historic Site. National Park Service. U.S. Department of the Interior.

Fort Concho-National Historic Landmark.

Fort Davis. National Park Service. U.S. Department of the Interior.

Fort Davis-July 1866: A Milestone in Black History. National Historic Site. National Park Service. U.S. Department of the Interior.

Fort Davis-The Buffalo Soldiers at Fort Davis 1867-1885. National Historic Site. National Park Service. U.S. Department of the Interior.

Fort Davis Retreat Parade Program. Southwest Parks and Monuments Association.

Goliad–A Place to Remember.

Gonzales Before and After the Alamo-It All Began Here. Gonzales, Texas: Gonzales Chamber of Commerce and Agriculture, n.d.

Gonzales County Historical Commission, ed. *Gonzales Before and After the Alamo–Walking Tour.* Gonzales, Texas: n.d.

Kendall, William T. *San Jacinto Battleground-State Historical Park.* n.p.: San Jacinto Museum of History and the Texas Parks and Wildlife Department, 1997.

Mehren House. San Antonio: n.d.

Nine Flags Over Goliad. n.p.: n.d.

OBanion, Maurine M. *The Battle of Plum Creek.* Lockhart, Texas: Lockhart Chamber of Commerce, n.d.

Palo Alto Battlefield. n.p.: U.S. Government Printing Office, 1994.✗

Presidio La Bahia-"Fort of the Bay." n.p.✗

Resaca de la Palma. Palo Alto Battlefield. National Historic Site. National Park Service. U.S. Department of the Interior.✗

Sabine Pass Battleground State Historical Park. n.p.: Texas Parks and Wildlife Department, 1996.

Sites of the U.S.-Mexican War in the Brownsville Area. Palo Alto Battlefield. National Historic Site. National Park Service. U.S. Department of the Interior.

Sterne-Hoya House. n.p.: Bruce Lyndon Cunningham Production, 1985.

Stone Fort Museum. Nacogdoches, Texas: n.d.

Visitors' & Newcomers' Guide. Gonzales, Texas.

Guide Books

Texas-Texas State Travel Guide. Austin: Texas Department of Transportation, n.d.

Texas Traveler. Austin: The Publishing Partnership, A Division of Texas Monthly, Inc., 1995.

Maps

Ham, Caiaphas K. *Battle of San Saba.*

Kendall, W.T. and Ronna Hurd. *The Battle of San Jacinto-A Map of the Battleground on April 21, 1836.* Texas: San Jacinto Museum of History, San Jacinto Monument, 1989.

The Military History of Texas Map! Norman, Oklahoma: Map Inc., 1996.

Texas. Washington D.C.: Cartographic Division, National Geographic Society, 1986.

Texas Official Highway Map. Texas Department of Transportation, 1993.

Newspapers

Barrick, Rick. "Karakawas Spelled Trouble." *Brazosport (Texas) Facts*, 28 March 1980.

Calliman, Elmer L. "The Indian Battle that Whipped Mexico." *Dallas Morning News*, 10 August 1930.

Case, Peggy. "Jones Creek Named as a Tribute to Indian Fighter." *Brazosport (Texas) Facts*, 4 November 1973.

Chapman, Art. "And the Walls Came Tumbling Down." *Fort Worth Star-Telegram*, 14 June 1992, Sec. E, 1.

Dixon, T.H. "A Frontier Incident–Particulars of the Tragic Affair on Battle Creek, Texas." n.d., n.p.

Ellis, Anna. "At the Salado the Mexican Invaders Suffered Defeat." *San Antonio Express*, 16 September 1934.

"Fight at Battle Creek." n.p., 26 September 1897.

Greer, J.K. "Texas' Biggest Fight with the Indians." *Dallas Morning News*, 8 January 1928.

Hayward, Susana. "'Angel of the Alamo' given overdue honor." *San Antonio Express-News*. 9 September 1997, 1(A) and 4(A).

_____. "Santa Anna Makes His Mark Again." *San Antonio Express-News*. 18 September 1997, 1(A) and 6(A).

LaRoche, Clarence J. "Corpus Christi: 'The Vicksburg of Texas.'" *San Antonio Express-News*, 7 March 1965.

Markley, Melanie. "Fort Velasco Site 'Digging' Stirs Up New Interest in Area." *Brazosport (Texas) Facts*, 28 December 1980.

Maverick, Maury. "Forgotten Slave a True Hero." *San Antonio Express-News*, 23 June 1991.

_____. "Out-of-the-Way Historical Sites." *San Antonio Express-News*, 24 February 1991.

"Packsaddle Indian Fight 111th Anniversary." *Llano (Texas) News*, 2 August 1984.

Rogers, Marjorie. "Early Texas Surveyors Victims of Massacre by Indians in 1838." 15 November 1936. n.p.

"Tales of Texas - Some Indian Fights which occurred in Navarro County." n.p., n.d.

Unpublished Material
Bowser, David. "Notes on the Battle of the Salado." San Antonio, 1990.
Looscan, Adele B. "The Old Mexican Fort at Velasco." Brazoria County Historical Museum.
Nelson, George. "Background of Col. Juan De Ugalde."
_____. "Bicentennial of Colonel Juan de Ugalde's Victory." Uvalde County Historical Commission.

Index

229

Index

Other Books from Republic of Texas Press

100 Days in Texas: The Alamo Letters
by Wallace O. Chariton

Alamo Movies
by Frank Thompson

A Cowboy of the Pecos
by Patrick Dearen

A Treasury of Texas Trivia
by Bill Cannon

Alamo Movies
by Frank Thompson

At Least 1836 Things You Ought to Know About Texas but Probably Don't
by Doris L. Miller

Battlefields of Texas
by Bill Groneman

Best Tales of Texas Ghosts
by Docia Schultz Williams

Bubba Speak: A Texas Dictionary
by W.C. Jameson

Civil War Recollections of James Lemuel Clark and the Great Hanging at Gainesville, Texas in October 1862
by L.D. Clark

Cow Pasture Pool: Golf on the Muni-tour
by Joe D. Winter

Cripple Creek Bonanza
by Chet Cunningham

Daughter of Fortune: The Bettie Brown Story
by Sherrie S. McLeRoy

Defense of a Legend: Crockett and the de la Peña Diary
by Bill Groneman

Don't Throw Feathers at Chickens: A Collection of Texas Political Humor
by Charles Herring, Jr. and Walter Richter

Other Books from Republic of Texas Press

Eight Bright Candles: Courageous Women of Mexico
by Doris E. Perlin

Etta Place: Her Life and Times with Butch Cassidy and the Sundance Kid
by Gail Drago

Exiled: The Tigua Indians of Ysleta del Sur
by Randy Lee Eickhoff

Exploring Dallas with Children: A Guide for Family Activities (2nd Ed.)
by Kay McCasland Threadgill

Exploring San Antonio with Children: A Guide for Family Activities
by Docia Schultz Williams

Exploring the Alamo Legends
by Wallace O. Chariton

Eyewitness to the Alamo
by Bill Groneman

First in the Lone Star State
by Sherrie S. McLeRoy

The Funny Side of Texas
by Ellis Posey and John Johnson

Ghosts Along the Texas Coast
by Docia Schultz Williams

The Great Texas Airship Mystery
by Wallace O. Chariton

Henry Ossian Flipper: West Point's First Black Graduate
by Jane Eppinga

Horses and Horse Sense: The Practical Science of Horse Husbandry
by James "Doc" Blakely

How the Cimarron River Got Its Name and Other Stories About Coffee
by Ernestine Sewell Linck

The Last Great Days of Radio
by Lynn Woolley

Other Books from Republic of Texas Press

The Last of the Old-Time Cowboys
by Patrick Dearen

Letters Home: A Soldier's Legacy
by Roger L. Shaffer

More Wild Camp Tales
by Mike Blakely

Noble Brutes: Camels on the American Frontier
by Eva Jolene Boyd

Outlaws in Petticoats and Other Notorious Texas Women
by Gail Drago and Ann Ruff

Phantoms of the Plains: Tales of West Texas Ghosts
by Docia Schultz Williams

Rainy Days in Texas Funbook
by Wallace O. Chariton

Red River Women
by Sherrie S. McLeRoy

The Return of the Outlaw Billy the Kid
by W.C. Jameson and Fredric Bean

The Santa Fe Trail
by James A. Crutchfield

Slitherin' 'Round Texas
by Jim Dunlap

Spindletop Unwound
by Roger L. Shaffer

Spirits of San Antonio and South Texas
by Docia Schultz Williams and Reneta Byrne

The Star Film Ranch: Texas' First Picture Show
by Frank Thompson

Tales of the Guadalupe Mountains
by W.C. Jameson

The Texas Golf Guide
by Art Stricklan

Other Books from Republic of Texas Press

Texas Highway Humor
by Wallace O. Chariton

Texas Politics in My Rearview Mirror
by Waggoner Carr and Byron Varner

Texas Ranger Tales: Stories That Need Telling
by Mike Cox

Texas Tales Your Teacher Never Told You
by Charles F. Eckhardt

Texas Wit and Wisdom
by Wallace O. Chariton

That Cat Won't Flush
by Wallace O. Chariton

That Old Overland Stagecoaching
by Eva Jolene Boyd

This Dog'll Hunt
by Wallace O. Chariton

To the Tyrants Never Yield: A Texas Civil War Sampler
by Kevin R. Young

Tragedy at Taos: The Revolt of 1847
by James A. Crutchfield

A Trail Rider's Guide to Texas
by Mary Elizabeth Sue Goldman

A Treasury of Texas Trivia
by Bill Cannon

Unsolved Texas Mysteries
by Wallace O. Chariton

Western Horse Tales
Edited by Don Worcester

When Darkness Falls: Tales of San Antonio Ghosts and Hauntings
by Docia Schultz Williams

Wild Camp Tales
by Mike Blakely